Eastside Story

East side Story

Steven C. Thedford

New World Press, Inc
NEXT LEVEL PUBLISHING

New World Press, Inc
NEXT LEVEL PUBLISHING

Copyright 2021 by Steven C. Thedford
All rights reserved. For information about permission to reproduce selections from this book, please write to Permissions, New World Press, Inc.
5626 Platte Dr., Ellenwood, GA 30294
ISBN: 978-0975973097
Library of Congress Control Number: 2021949594
Printed in the United States of America

This book is dedicated to Ms. Ashley Coleman, a 2004 graduate of Redan High School, who suggested that we write this book in fifth-period Physical Science class.

CHAPTER 1

On February 23, 1895, the Illinois Club of New Orleans held the first official African American debutante ball at the Globe Hall on St. Peter and Maris Street in New Orleans, Louisiana. On that night, the organization introduced the crescent city to the most gorgeous, charming, and genteel women of color. The ball took place around 10:00 p.m. The maids and butlers had to finish their day job before attending the event. Debutantes wore beautiful white gowns and headpieces with feathers of assorted colors—red, orange, yellow, and black.

As a young girl, Egypt James heard the story of her mother's debutante ball so often that she vowed to never be a debutante. On their weekly shopping trips to the mall, Mrs. James would just go on and on about how much she loved waltzing, waving in flowing gowns, and wearing tiaras at her Carnival Ball. When

Egypt entered high school, she started ignoring her mother's claims that the ball gave the young ladies' confidence and a sense of worth, provided cultural reinforcement, scholarships, and allowed women to network. But for Egypt, the balls were "pretentious" and only meant for girls from well-to-do families.

However, at a summer camp in Charlotte, North Carolina, Egypt's counselor changed her mind about being a debutante. Her camp counselor had been a debutante, and Egypt was impressed how confidently she sang the national anthem at the opening of camp. After having several late-night conversations with her about the benefits of the year-long program, Egypt finally wrote a letter to her mother from the camp expressing her desire to become a debutante. Mrs. James was more than excited and placed a few phone calls to the Southern Ladies Sorority of Stone Mountain, Georgia, an African American organization dedicated to uplifting young ladies of color for almost one hundred years. They accepted Egypt as a debutante for the upcoming year and invited her to the first event, a cotillion tea.

Egypt returned home from the camp a few days before the event. Her mother told Egypt to tell people that she had been attending an academic camp in Massachusetts and not that she was receiving treatment for mental exhaustion. She did not want the selection committee for the sorority to know the truth. For the event, Mrs. James made Egypt try out several dresses. But Egypt hated most of them. They reminded her of the outfits that women wore in Antebellum. But she tried not to complain too much as she didn't want to seem ungrateful. As Egypt stood in front of a full-length mirror in her bedroom, trying on one of the dresses, her grandmother walked into the room holding the most beautiful dress that she had ever seen—a rushed cocktail dress that had a jasmine hem shaded in blue.

Egypt's face gleamed. "Whose dress is that?"

Egypt's grandmother smiled and said, "Yours."

"Can I wear it to the cotillion tea?"

"Sure," replied her grandmother.

Egypt looked over to her mother and said, "Mom…"

"Don't worry about hurting my feelings," interjected Mrs. James. "I like the dress too. You'll look beautiful in it."

* * *

An hour before the cotillion tea, the members of the Southern Ladies of Stone Mountain were busy setting up tables. Some of them had spent all night folding napkins for the guests. Each table was covered with a white tablecloth, cutlery, plates, saucers, teacups, and napkins. The ladies were about to finish when the lights went out.

Several women screamed. The director picked up her smartphone and turned on the flashlight app. She shined the light around the room until she found the door. As she walked in that direction, other women also turned on their flashlight apps.

Everyone sighed in relief as the lights came back on. A few minutes later, the director walked back in. "What happened?" inquired one of the sorority members.

"We have too many teapots plugged in," replied the director. The women laughed. "Take one of the teapots to my office."

One of the ladies unplugged a teapot and started to move it to another room but spilled the water. They looked at one another and then all looked toward the door. Egypt, one of the debutantes, stood there holding her dress in one hand; her stilettos hung from her fingers on the other.

"Wow!" the director uttered. "You are beautiful."

"Thank you," said Egypt as she stood in the doorway, blushing in embarrassment while the ladies whispered to one another about her beauty.

"Do you need any help?" asked Egypt.

"We could use some assistance cleaning up this mess," said the director.

Egypt hung up her dress and shoes in the closet. She walked to the bathroom to get some paper towels and bumped into another debutante.

"I didn't know you were going to be here," said India as her eyes widened. She was staring in the mirror and putting on mascara.

Egypt scrunched her forehead, raised an eyebrow, and pursed her lips together. "I could say the same of you."

India put down her mascara brush and stared at Egypt. "What's that supposed to mean?"

"You just don't seem like a girl who would like . . . to dress."

"What are you trying to say?"

Egypt took a deep breath. "I don't have the time for this. I promised to help clean up." She grabbed a bunch of paper towels and left India in the bathroom.

As Egypt cleaned up the water, more debutantes began to arrive. Some were chatting, but most pulled out their cell phones and started texting and playing games. After finishing her task,

Egypt left with her clothes. The director walked to the podium and made an announcement. "Turn in all cell phones to me in the front of the room." The girls got up and walked to the podium. One of the ladies gave each girl a sticky note. The debutantes wrote their names and placed the notes on their phones as they dropped them into a box, then went back to their seats. The director walked onto the stage and looked over the program. Egypt appeared at the door with her blue dress, earrings, lip gloss, white gloves, stilettos, purse flung over her left shoulder, and African braids in a crown bun, and an amulet of Bastet—the goddess of protection—hanging around her neck.

"She looks like Nyakim Gatwech," said a debutante. Egypt blushed and walked to her seat as the women buzzed with conversation. The director pounded her gavel several times, and the room grew quiet.

"Good morning," said the director. "Welcome to the Southern Ladies of Stone Mountain, GA debutante class."

The ladies in the room clapped.

"This year you will be involved in several events that will help you prepare for the final event of the year, the debutante ball, including the father-daughter dance, where your fathers will introduce into society."

Egypt began wheezing and coughing as the director continued. "Thus, this year you will have a tea today, classes on etiquette, and lunch at some of the best restaurants in Atlanta." Before she could finish, Egypt fell to the floor. The ladies rushed to her aid.

A sorority member who was a nurse directed the girls to give Egypt some air. As Egypt struggled to breathe, she pointed to her purse, which had fallen next to her. The nurse picked it up, unzipped it, and pulled out an inhaler. She gave it to Egypt, who took a few puffs. After a few moments, she began to breathe normally again.

"Are you OK?" asked the nurse.

"Yes, I get excited in new environments," lied Egypt.

The nurse helped Egypt back into her seat. "The emergency room is across the street. Do you want me to take you?"

"No," replied Egypt as she made sure her gloves were on correctly and smoothed out her dress. "I'll be fine now that I have my inhaler."

The debutantes and ladies returned to their seats, and the director continued to discuss the program.

"A list of activities is in the program book on your table. Please take this time to review the contents." The girls flipped through the program. Egypt took a few sips of water and looked around to see if anyone was watching her.

"We are about to eat," said the director. The girls straightened their big white hats and pulled down their bracelets. Egypt's stomach growled as she glanced over at the food on the trays—cucumber sandwiches, scones, breads, tarts, biscuits, vegetables, and meats. "Please, enjoy the tea."

As the girls got something to eat, the sorority ladies grabbed the tea and started serving. They poured the tea into porcelain cups. Before Egypt could get up, the director came over and served her. "The steam from the tea can help you with your asthma," she said as she sat down.

Egypt breathed in some of the steam, and it seemed to clear her airways. "I can breathe better. Where did you get this tea?"

The director poured her some tea in a cup and took a sip. "I got it from Africa on my last mission trip."

"What country did you visit?"

The director pointed to the black, green, and red pendant with a spear and shield around her neck. "Kenya."

"Do they have tea parties there?"

"The entire country stops for teatime at ten-thirty a.m.," said the director as one of the ladies brought Egypt and the director an assortment of foods. "Thank you."

"Including the schools?" asked Egypt before she took a bite of a cucumber sandwich.

"Yes," replied the director as she picked up a scone. "They serve tea with milk, bread, and butter."

Egypt ate some carrots and broccoli. "I've never had tea with milk before."

"Would you like some?"

"Yes," replied Egypt, and she took another bite of her sandwich.

The director walked to the tea table, picked up a small pitcher, and brought it to Egypt's table, while the other ladies engaged in teatime with the debutantes, talking about the tea and eating cucumber sandwiches and scones.

"I think you'll like it this way," said the director as she poured some milk into Egypt's tea.

"Yes, ma'am," said Egypt. "Can I have some sugar too?"

"Sure." The director dropped two sugar cubes in the tea,

and they splashed as they hit the surface of the beverage. Egypt began to cry.

"Are you having another attack?"

Egypt shook her head as tears rolled down her face.

"What is it?"

Egypt was silent for a moment. The last time she went to a tea party was when she was nine years old. She and her daddy were supposed to go to the zoo that day, but when her best friend asked her to go to a tea party, Egypt canceled their date

"I'm OK," said Egypt as she wiped her eyes. "I'm remembering the last time I had a tea party with my friend Aaliyah, and I . . ."

"You miss her?"

"Uh-huh," mumbled Egypt, trying to convince the director.

"We all miss friends from our childhood, but you'll make new ones this year."

Egypt forced a smile, hoping that her story was believable. The director gave Egypt a hug and walked back to the podium. She said a few parting words and dismissed the girls.

Egypt was about to get up when India approached her. "That was a nice act, but I see right through you."

"What are you talking about?" asked Egypt as the sorority ladies cleaned the room.

"Getting the director to feel sorry for you."

"I didn't—"

"Don't even try it. You've got this innocent, genteel act down pat, trying to win the scholarship competition."

"I don't know what you're talking about."

"Watch your back!"

Chapter 2

It took Egypt several attempts, but she finally fought off the sleepy monster and woke up from her morning nap. She sat up on the orange benches in front of the Stone Mountain community center and couldn't believe what she saw: the drum major spraying laundry detergent on her car. She raced toward her Volkswagen Bug and tried to grab the water hose, but the boys were too tall; she couldn't jump high enough to grab it. She gave up on that strategy but grabbed the bucket of suds from Paris, her best friend. The girls struggled until Paris dumped the contents on Egypt's head.

"I can't believe you just did that," Egypt gasped as she stood there with suds dripping from her braids, like a wet mop. "Your bouncy curls are next."

Egypt chased Paris around her car, but she couldn't quite catch her. After running several laps around the Volkswagen Bug, the girls came to a standstill with Egypt at the front of the car and Paris at the back.

Egypt took a couple of deep breaths. "Love, I will get you."

"Not if you can't catch me."

The director walked up to the girls, and they snapped to attention. She gave them an order. "Go work the corner!"

"Sure," said Egypt, but she whispered to Paris, "What kind of girl does she think I am?"

Paris chuckled. "We have to collect money in front of the center."

"Oh."

Egypt, in her blue flip-flops, jean shorts, and a blue midriff shirt, walked to the front of the recreation center along with Paris, determined to collect donations for the youth group. She held up a big sign with both hands that read "Car Wash Donations." Cars sped through the intersection so fast that they never saw the sign, so Egypt started waiting until the light turned red before trying to convince drivers to donate. She walked in front of the cars like a ring girl at a boxing match, and the male drivers dropped their donations into the bucket.

After about two hours, the director signaled for Egypt and Paris to come back to the parking lot, where kids were still washing cars. As the girls walked toward the bus lane, they ran into two other band members, India and Stephen, who were replacing them on the corner. Paris handed Stephen her sign, but India snatched it from Egypt.

"That was rude," snapped Egypt.

India rolled her eyes. "I still have my eye on you, chocolate girl."

"Are you still mad about what happened at the cotillion tea?" asked Egypt as Paris pulled her toward the community center.

"No," said India as she headed to the street with Stephen.

"What is she talking about?" asked Paris.

"The cotillion tea," replied Egypt.

"The thing you tried to get me to join?"

"Yeah."

"I don't have time for tea parties and stuff like that . . . I have to study."

"Love, there's a problem."

"What?"

"I need my father for the last event of the year."

"How are you going to find him?"

"I don't know yet."

About this time Egypt and Paris reached the center.

The girls fumbled through the donation bucket and noticed several small pieces of paper and a business card. Egypt slipped the card into her pocket. Egypt's father used to give her his business cards, which had "LD03" and his name printed on them, to play with in church to keep her quiet during the service. Afterward, she picked up a few of the notes from the bucket, read them, and laughed.

"Why are these people writing you notes?" asked Egypt.

"I think they're for you," replied Paris.

"How do you know that?"

Paris unfolded a couple of the notes and read them. "'Do you want to be a dancer at my club, the Gallery?' 'You look good enough to eat.' 'I can get you a star on the walk of fame.'"

"They could be for you," said Egypt.

Paris looked at Egypt with an incredulous stare. "Not with those booty shorts you're wearing."

"They're not too short," said Egypt as she tried to pull them down.

"You look like a professional."

Egypt hit Paris with a playful tap. "No, I don't."

"We could get paid," said Paris as she handed the bucket to the director, who instructed them to help the other youth members. Egypt sprayed tire cleaner on the tires, and streaks of filth rolled down. Egypt grabbed a brush from a bucket of soapy water and scrubbed. When she finished, Paris rinsed the tires with the hose.

Egypt and Paris worked so hard for an hour that they earned a break and went over to the flea market that was set up on the sidewalk. Egypt bought a pickle and a bottle of spring water. Paris grabbed a honey bun and a grape soda.

The girls walked over to Egypt's car and sat down in front of it. Egypt tore the plastic from the top of the pickle bag and bit off a chunk. Paris ate her snack and gulped down her grape soda.

Egypt unscrewed the top of her water bottle and took a couple of sips. She squeezed her fingers into her jeans pocket, pulled out the business card, and started dialing the number printed on it.

Paris almost choked. "What are you doing?"

"Dialing a number," Egypt said.

Paris tried to grab the phone. "Stranger danger!" screamed Paris. "Hang up before somebody answers!"

"Hey," said a voice on the other end of the line. Egypt stared at Paris for a moment before finally speaking. "Hello."

"Who's this?"

"Egypt."

"How did you get my number?"

"You gave it to me."

"When?"

"Today."

The caller was quiet for a few moments before asking, "Are you the girl with the hoochie mama shorts?"

"Yes," said Egypt, but she didn't like to be called that. "What's your name?"

"William Harris," said the caller. "Do you go to Eastside High School?"

"No," replied Egypt. Paris broke free from the wrestling hold.

"I knew I hadn't seen you in the halls."

Egypt hesitated for a minute, trying to figure out what Paris was about to do. "I attend a private school." Egypt neglected to tell William that she was thrown out of her school and her mother had enrolled her in Eastside High School.

"Can I come back up to the recreation center to visit you?"

"Sure," said Egypt.

Paris charged. Egypt moved out of the way, and Paris bumped her head on Egypt's car. Egypt put her hand over her mouth to keep from laughing into the phone. She gathered her composure and asked William, "What will you be driving?"

"A red motorcycle."

"When are you coming?"

"In about thirty minutes," said William, and he hung up the phone.

Egypt joined Paris, who was sitting next to her car, rubbing her head. "I can't believe you did that," said Paris.

"Me either."

"So why did you do it?"

"Blame it on my teenage brain."

"I think we should go help clean up." Paris pointed to the youth members who had started the process.

"You're right," said Egypt. So they headed toward the bus lane to help.

Egypt poured the dirty suds into the street while Paris pulled the hose to the back of the building. Afterward, Egypt and Paris picked up water bottles and cans until Paris pointed to a motorcycle turning into the parking lot. William pulled up to the curb next to Egypt, music blasting. Egypt pointed to her ear, indicating that she couldn't hear. So William turned off his radio and his motorcycle.

"Hello," said William as he removed his helmet, displaying a squashed-box haircut, a thin, muscular build, and a brown-paper-bag complexion. He stepped off his bike and walked toward Egypt, towering over her. She looked into his light-brown almond eyes and became entranced by his smile, which showed all his white teeth.

Paris nudged Egypt. "Say something."

"I thought you didn't want me to talk to him," said Egypt, looking back at William.

"He's cute."

"What should I say?"

"Just talk to him."

Egypt turned her attention to William. "You have a nice motorcycle."

"Would you like a ride?"

"My mother told me never to go with strangers."

"If we go on a date, we won't be."

"I can't go out until I'm sixteen."

"When is that?"

"In October."

"You don't have to tell anybody."

Egypt slammed her phone against William's motorcycle helmet. "Why are you trying to talk to me like I'm some low-budget girl?"

"Yikes! You're high maintenance. I'm outta here." William climbed onto his motorcycle and left. He skidded, popped a wheelie, sped down the street, and disappeared.

Paris walked up to Egypt and asked, "You enjoyed the rush?"

"Yeah," said Egypt, "but if we ever go out . . . I'll have to train him."

Egypt and Paris walked toward Egypt's car, as Paris put her hand in front of her face.

"You need the sun, with your light skin," said Egypt with a grin as she saw her reflection in Paris's glasses and pulled her friend's hand down.

Paris pushed Egypt's hands away. "All of us don't have a perfect onyx complexion like you."

An ice-cream truck pulled into the parking lot and filled the air with a melody of songs that brought kids running. "Does that ice cream truck sell strawberry shortcake ice cream bars?" Egypt asked.

"The LD03 sells that and anything else you want," said Paris as she turned up her nose.

Egypt stopped and reached down into her pants. She pulled

out William's business card and noticed that it had LD03 embossed on it.

"What's the LD03?" asked Egypt.

Paris said, "It's a gang that sells drugs and helps girls at Eastside become dancers at the local teen club, the Gallery."

"I want to be a dancer!"

"Not *that* kind."

Chapter 3

"Cease all activities and stand for the Pledge of Allegiance," ordered the chief petty officer of the Eastside High School ROTC over the intercom. Students in Mr. G's physical science class stopped in their tracks as they listened to the officer's voice echo. Afterward, they returned to their disruptive activities, refusing to follow instructions and chasing each other around the room.

The clinking of keys stopped the foolishness. The security guard, who was as tall as a redwood tree, wearing clothes that were too little for him, had stepped in. The boys rushed to their seats because they didn't want to get into trouble.

Mr. G reminded his students of TI the rapper, but with a bald spot in the back of his head. He tried to cover it up with a haircut that made him look bald. He always wore nice dress pants, a white button-down shirt with a tie, and leather shoes. Mr. G started each class with a smile, but by the end of the day his eyelids would droop, his nose would become wrinkly, and his upper lip would be raised.

Mr. G used to teach in Africa at a school called Mbeji Academy in Ng'iya, Kenya, about 50 kilometers from the Uganda border. He had never thought about being a teacher before until the Global Foundation of Education had offered him the opportunity to teach in East Africa while he was in college. The students in Kenya had so much respect for teachers that Mr. G decided that he would become an educator when he returned to the States. So, he applied for a teaching position at Eastside High School in Stone Mountain, GA, but he was in for a rude awakening.

As the announcements began, Mr. G fumbled through a pile of papers on his desk, trying to find his lesson plans. The students gossiped and joked around while Egypt read her Bible.

Paris tapped Egypt on her shoulder. "I still can't believe your mother let you transfer to Eastside High School."

"Me either," said Egypt.

"How did you do it?" asked Paris.

"She kept saying no, but I wore her down."

"What did you do?"

"I told her that I needed to be around real people, not the spoiled kids in private schools."

"That worked?"

"Not at first, but after a couple of days she gave in."

"I'm just glad that we will be going to school together."

"Me too."

"Did you ask your mother about finding your father?"

"I tried, but she got really mad; I left that alone."

As the intercom went quiet, the class grew silent. The hairs on the back of Mr. G's neck stood up. He pushed the white emergency button on the wall and sat back down. After a few seconds, an administrator appeared in his doorway.

"That was fast," said Mr. G.

The administrator caught his breath and bent over with his hands on his knees. "I used to be a state champion back in the day."

"With that beer belly?" called out William. The class burst out laughing.

The administrator had been smiling but regained his composure. "What's the problem?"

"The students are acting crazy."

"More than usual?"

"Yeah."

The administrator looked across the classroom until he came to the last row of students. His eyes searched each facial expression until he came to a male student wearing a black muscle shirt with no sleeves. The student had a tattoo on the upper part of his arm that said "LD03." The administrator walked over to the student and picked up a pen on the student's desk. He pulled off the top of the writing instrument. A three-inch blade appeared.

The class gasped.

The administrator held up the blade. "Is this yours?" he demanded.

The student didn't respond. He just sat and stared into space with a blank look on his face. After several attempts to get the student to acknowledge him, the administrator pulled his radio from his belt and called the resource officer, who arrived a short time thereafter.

"Get up," said the resource officer, but the student sat firmly rooted in his seat. The officer's face grew red, and he made a sweeping motion with his arm. "OK, everybody out!" he bellowed. As the students filed out of the room, the resource officer pulled out his can of mace and shook it several times high in the air.

Egypt was almost through the door but stopped just before the officer pressed the button to spray the student. "I am a student counselor at the youth group that meets every Saturday morning at the community center, and we help students make good decisions. I think I can get him to move."

The officer paused for a moment. "You have two minutes; otherwise, he's going to jail."

Egypt walked up to the student, closed her eyes, and whispered into his ear. He got up from his seat and hugged her. Then he walked out of the room. The officer had to run to catch him.

"What did you say to him?" asked the administrator.

"Please get up for me," replied Egypt.

"How did you know that would work?"

"He smiles at me all the time."

The administrator walked out of the class. The students walked back into the room and returned to their seats. Egypt and Paris sat down.

"I like your dress," said Paris.

"Thank you," replied Egypt.

"Is it your mother's?"

"Love, my mother wishes she could get in my dress."

Mr. G started collecting the homework. When he turned his back, the students shot spit balls into the tiles on the ceiling, dumped pinecones into the fish tank, drew elaborate graffiti on the desks with permanent markers, and stuffed their faces with the chicken biscuits the National Honor Society had sold before school.

William hollered, "Can I go to the bathroom?"

"No!" replied Mr. G.

India had been sleeping in class, but the noise woke her up. She lifted her head and screamed, "Shut up!" Then she went back to sleep.

William put a pencil down the back of Egypt's beaded black dress and tapped the metal closure of her bra several times till it unfastened.

"Oh my God!" Egypt grabbed her chest, jumped up, and rushed out of the room.

Paris Thomas ran after her in her blue polo shirt and French Toast girls plain skirt that she wore at her private school, before she transferred to Eastside High School. Her parents wanted her to attend the best schools so that she would get accepted into Harvard University. But by the time she entered high school, Mr. and Mrs. Thomas could no longer afford the private school tuition. So, they sent Paris to Eastside High School, which had one of the best science programs in Stone Mountain.

Mr. G saw Egypt's ebony legs flying out of the door. He looked at William and knew he had done something. "Get out!" he screamed.

"I needed to go to the bathroom anyway," William retorted. He entered the hall and came upon a female student wearing a brown top, a brown mini skirt, and brown high heels that were so high she swayed like a skyscraper. Her purse was on the floor in front of her. William couldn't figure out why she hadn't picked it up, but he soon realized that she didn't want to bend down and show all of God's glory to the world. William helped her out; he picked up her pocketbook and handed it to her before he headed to the bathroom.

The stench of urine almost knocked William out when he walked into the comfort station. Nobody cleaned the boys' restroom, and the boys missed the target too often. He almost left, but he could hear the scurrying of feet in the stalls. As he rounded the corner, he saw two guys standing in front of the handicapped stall looking like security guards at a nightclub with LD03 tattoos on their arms, and two other guys on their knees throwing dice.

The security detail cleared their throats, and the guys in the stall stopped playing. A short guy named John, with a short afro, a light skin, and bloodshot eyes, approached William, stopping inches from his chin. William stood his ground. He stared at John for a few moments. Nobody in the bathroom said a word.

John Adebayo rose in the leadership of the LD03 gang organization after an administrator at Eastside High School recruited him. On a teacher workday, John showed up to the school for class and was so strung out on drugs that he had no idea the students didn't have to report. John had been staying with friends for sexual favors since middle school; one day he came home, and his parents were gone. Once the administrator, a member of the gang, heard John's story he offered him a family, the LD03.

John put his balled fist up to his mouth and mumbled, "How can I help you?"

William handed John an LD03 business card with the name "Baba" on it. He looked at it and turned it over. "He's good," he said to his boys.

"Can I join the activities?" asked William.

"I don't know if you can afford us."

William pulled a wad of cash out of his jeans, just enough for John and his boys to see.

"Let's play."

William and John entered the bathroom stall. John handed the dice over to William, allowing him to bet five dollars that he would roll a seven or an eleven. William shook the dice and threw them against the toilet. They landed on the floor, a three and a four.

John and his boys threw their hands up in the air in disgust. "Beginner's luck," said John.

"I'm just getting started, shawty."

William passed again with a five-dollar bet and rolled an eleven.

John grabbed William and pushed him up against the wall. "I'm tired of you," he said through his teeth.

"Yikes! You're the strongest little man I know," said William.

"Don't make fun of me!" yelled John. "My nerves are bad when I don't have my joint in the morning."

"What happened? Why didn't you have your joint?"

"Somebody stole our ice cream truck."

A man cleared his throat, and all the boys turned their heads to see the discipline administrator staring at them.

"Young men, please come with me."

Chapter 4

The security guard parked his golf cart in front of trailer nine, leaned back, closed his eyes, and fell asleep. Three members of the LD03 gang—John, Caleb, and Sam—wearing do-rags and sunglasses, sneaked up on the guard from behind. Caleb and Sam held a piece of wood in their hands the size of a door and moved around to the front of the golf cart. They leaned the wood so it touched the ground and the roof of the cart.

John reached around the waist of the security guard and pulled out his radio, and a skateboarder hit the ramp and flew over the guard's head, which woke him up. He reached for his radio, but it was no longer on his belt. John, Caleb, and Sam took off running. The guard pressed on the pedal and flew after the LD03 members as they ran down the sidewalk. His cart almost turned over as he turned the corner.

As soon as the security guard disappeared, skateboarders and students filed into the areas in front of the trailers. The students set up several ramps so they could see their classmates perform. Caleb had gotten away from the guard and broke through the crowd. He grabbed a skateboard from a student just before he was about to take off. They started to boo him, but when he performed a drop-in, a backside kick turn, a frontside kick turn, and finished off his performance with a frontside one-eighty, they all cheered.

Paris opened the door to Mr. G's trailer. She carried her lunch on a tray, two pieces of the pepperoni deep-dish pizza that had been delivered from the local pizzeria, corn on the cob, a small salad with dressing, and a piece of yellow cake with chocolate frosting in a small plastic container. Paris, wearing a light blue polo shirt and French Toast girl's stretch pants, walked over to a desk and sat down next to her best friend.

Egypt took a bite of her turkey sandwich on rye bread with lettuce, tomato, and Miracle Whip. "How did you get through the crowd?" asked Egypt.

"I went the back way," said Paris as she wiped the sweat from her forehead.

Egypt handed Paris some hand sanitizer.

"Thank you," said Paris.

"Are you going to eat all that?" asked Egypt with a look of amazement on her face.

Paris glared at her. "I didn't eat breakfast."

"My mother made me pancakes, again."

Paris stuffed a piece of pizza in her mouth. "I wish my parents had time to do that." Paris's family use to spend time together going to Stone Mountain Park and plays, but once her parents got promotions, her father and mother had to spend more time at work.

"You know why?" asked Egypt.

"I do," said Paris, finishing off her chocolate milk. "She still won't tell you anything about why your father left?"

"Nope," said Egypt as she took another bite of her sandwich.

"Keep asking her; she'll break sooner or later."

"Love, I hope so."

"Have you thought about what you are going to do if you can't find your father for the dance at the debutante ball?" asked Paris.

"Not really."

Egypt's phone rang and she picked it up. "Hello."

"Can you talk?" asked Mrs. James.

"Yes," replied Egypt.

"Mr. G sent me an email that you ran out of class. What was that about?"

"Nothing. William caused a wardrobe malfunction.

"Who is William?"

"A boy Mr. G hates."

"We'll talk more about this when you get home," said Egypt's mom. "I found the cutest skirt for you while I was shopping during lunch. "Do you want it?"

"Sure."

"Is Paris there?"

"Yes, Mom."

"Tell her I said hi."

"I will," said Egypt

There was a long pause on the phone. "Mom, is there something else you wanted to tell me?"

"Your cousin Sagmus is going to stay with us for a while," said Mrs. James.

"Why?" asked Egypt as she raised her voice a little.

"Her parents think that their overseas missionary trips are starting to affect Sagmus's education and behavior," replied Mrs. James.

"Sagmus is a handful," said Egypt.

"You're right. The church told Sagmus's parents that she couldn't come on any more missionary trips because she caused too much trouble with the children in the villages that they were trying to help; she played too many practical jokes on them."

"What am I supposed to do with her?"

"Think of Sagmus as the little sister you never had."

Egypt twisted her braids. "Can we talk about this later?"

"Yes, but I have to get back to court to defend my client," said Mrs. James as she hung up.

As Egypt ended the phone call with her mother, she noticed that Paris's cell phone was in her calculator case.

"Love, why is your phone in there?"

"I lost my case," said Paris but she didn't tell Egypt the truth. The smart students at Eastside High School taught her that it was "better to cheat than repeat." Her parents expected her to get the best grades. Any mark below an A was considered a failure. Also, she didn't want her best friend to know how she got her straight As. Paris used her cell phone to look up the answers on the test so she could get the grades to attend an Ivy League school.

Paris stared at Egypt's amulet, a woman in an Egyptian head-dress, a hair of horns, and a sun disk, which she thought was the most beautiful piece of jewelry she had ever seen.

Mr. G walked toward the girls as he ate a baked potato that had a touch of salt, a slice of butter on top, and melted cheddar cheese topped with chives, and bacon bits.

"That's so cheesy," said Egypt.

Before he could sit down, the trio heard a huge commotion coming from the trailer next door. Egypt, Paris, and Mr. G bolted out of the trailer. They saw an enormous crowd in the doorway of trailer nine. They tried to see through the crowd, but there were so many people that it looked more like the teenage club, the Gallery, on a Saturday night after a football game. Mr. G forced his way into the walkway and parted the students where he heard whooping and hollering.

Egypt started to follow but remembered that trailer nine had a musty smell that wouldn't quit. The janitors did the best they could to get rid of the smell, but the odor from the track team had been grounded into the carpet. As the students' voices got louder, Egypt mustered the courage to go into the portable classroom.

She couldn't believe her eyes.

Stephen had Mr. G elevated above his head, carrying him around the room. Mr. G.'s eyes were as big as pool balls as the rest of the class laughed.

Egypt caught up with Stephen and Mr. G. She stared at his face. "Put Mr. G. down!"

Stephen took a deep breath to focus on the request. He had trouble concentrating on his words; he'd suffered a traumatic brain injury in a car crash.. As a result of the accident, he had been under the care of the special education department.

"I didn't mean to scare you," said Stephen as he sat Mr. G. on the carpet. "Sometimes I don't know my own strength."

Mr. G collected himself, stood up, and dusted himself off. "Thanks. I enjoyed the ride, and I know you were not trying to hurt me, but students, please go to lunch."

"We want to see the rest of the show," said William.

The sound of William's voice caused Mr. G's hands to tremble, eyes to glare, and lips to narrow. Mr. G hollered, "Now!"

"Yikes!" said William. "Teachers be flipping on a nig--!" William exited the trailer along with his classmates.

As the students left, the resource officer showed up, huffing and puffing.

"What took you so long?" asked Mr. G.

"Chasing the LD03," replied the security guard, as he stood bent over, trying to catch his breath. "I'm going to get those thugs if it is the last thing I do."

"Don't you ride in a golf cart?" asked Mr. G.

"Yes," replied the guard.

"Were you running after the boys?"

"No, I'm tired from running up the ramp."

Egypt, Paris, and Mr. G just looked at one another in amazement.

The security guard collected himself. "What's going on?"

Stephen raised his hand with a scared look on his face. "I'll tell you if I don't get in trouble." He knew that his case manager would be disappointed if he didn't tell the truth.

Egypt walked over to Stephen and gave him a hug. "Tell us what happened."

"Well, it all started with William," explained Stephen.

"I knew the LD03 had to be behind the whole thing," Egypt mumbled to herself.

Stephen wiped his tears from his face. "William laughed at me."

"Why?" asked Egypt.

"Because I got excited when I sat behind India."

"What did she do?"

"She . . . wore some red thongs," said Stephen, looking embarrassed.

Paris, the security guard, and Mr. G turned around so that Stephen didn't see them laughing.

"Why did you pick up Mr. G?" asked Egypt.

"I was trying to grab William because he stole my snack money, but Mr. G got in the way."

Students at Eastside High School made so much money selling snacks, cupcakes, chips, cookies, candy, and soft drinks, in class, the LDO3 took over the operation. Now the only way students could sell snacks was if they gave the gang a cut.

"Egypt, are you selling snacks at Eastside like everybody else?" asked Stephen.

"No," replied Egypt.

Stephen stared into Egypt's midnight eyes. "Your face favors Baba, the man who is over illegal snacks at Eastside High School."

"Love, where did you see him?"

"At the club, the Gallery."

Chapter 5

Egypt drove into the parking lot of Eastside High School as the LD03 gang members were throwing a football at one another. She couldn't find a student parking space, so she circled the parking lot several times, then pulled into a teacher's spot and put the car in park.

Egypt looked around the front of the school. "I wish Paris would hurry up," she said to herself as she sipped on the fruit smoothie her mother had made for her. She savored the aroma of the fresh strawberries from her mother's garden mixed with bananas, watermelon, and orange juice. Egypt leaned back on the headrest of her Volkswagen Bug. The sun had started to creep through the clouds, and Egypt drifted off to sleep.

A thump on the car woke her. Members of the LD03 had hit her car with the football.

Egypt jumped out of the car and looked down, praying that they had not dented her car; she knew that her mother wouldn't let her drive again if there was damage.

She didn't see any damage, but she did find the football; it had rolled under the car after striking it. She picked it up, gripped the ball around the laces, stood in a throwing stance, held it near her ear, and threw it in a circular motion, but the ball just flew straight up in the air. The other kids who had been standing around chatting with their friends and hugging one another fell out laughing.

Embarrassed, Egypt jumped into the car so fast that she couldn't even remember opening the door. She put her hands over her ears, face down on the steering wheel, trying to drown out the whooping and hollering of her classmates. Somebody knocked on the window; Egypt lifted her head and saw Paris.

"Love, I could kiss you," said Egypt as she opened the door.

"What happened?" asked Paris.

"I embarrassed myself, and I'm never going back to school."

Paris pushed up on her glasses. "You're overreacting."

"They're laughing at me," said Egypt with a frazzled look on her face.

Paris made Egypt look at the students continuing their morning rituals. "Whatever you did, they've forgotten about it. They're back to gossiping and being fresh with one another."

Egypt looked at the wall where students were gossiping and not paying attention to her anymore. "I think you're right." She wiped her eyes. "What took you so long?"

"I was trying to finish my breakfast," Paris said as she took a bite of her chicken biscuit. "The game will cheer you up."

"I hope so," said Egypt. "How did you find out about the game?"

"I get messages from the LD03."

"Why?"

"I dated one of them in ninth grade." Paris quickly showed Egypt the message on her phone.

"William sent me a message too."

"Who is the person on your wallpaper?" asked Paris.

" . . . My father," replied Egypt.

"He looks so familiar."

"Where do you know him from?"

"I can't remember, but it will come to me."

Egypt and Paris exited the car and walked over to the game. Enough players had arrived to form two teams: one from the North and one from the South. A crowd formed around the teams in the parking lot. Egypt couldn't understand why Paris wanted her to see the game.

The South boys were all born in Stone Mountain, Georgia, the east of the city of Atlanta. They took pride in the fact that they had never lost to the North boys, who were from Philadelphia or any area outside the South.

William Harris was originally from Philadelphia, where the schools were so bad that his father decided to send him to Georgia, a city ten miles east of Atlanta, to get a better education. Not only that, but his father could not accept the fact that his son was exploring his sexuality. Shipping him off to Atlanta helped him keep up his "street credit" from the LD03 gang members on the streets of "Philly." Yet, William was determined to gain his father's approval. He hoped that if he showed his father that he was tough, then he could come back home to help run the family's illegal business in "The City of Brotherly Love."

The South team broke the huddle. John caught the hike from the center and tried to pitch the ball to another player, but William intercepted the ball and ran it in for a touchdown. The North cheerleaders went crazy, jumping up and down.

"Why doesn't John's team have cheerleaders?" asked Egypt as William's team kicked the ball off to the LD03.

"Most girls of the LD03 are too cute to sweat, and they have to look good for entertaining after school, if you know what I mean," replied Paris.

Egypt started to argue but realized that Paris was right: She didn't want to get her Addison blouse and silk line skirt musty either.

For the first time in the history of Eastside, the South team trailed the North, and William started talking junk. "I thought boys from the South were tough."

John steamed as he barked out the signals for the next play. He dropped back to pass and pumped his arm, as if he had thrown the ball, but he tucked it under his arm and ran up the middle. When William saw John running, he stopped checking his man, chased John to the sidelines, and knocked him into the cheerleaders.

"What are you doing?" John said as he got to his feet. "This is touch football."

William bent over and put both hands on his knees, trying to catch his breath. "I was just trying to stop you."

In the next play, John acted as if he was going to run. William sprinted as fast as he could get to him, but just before he did, John threw a pass downfield to score the tying touchdown. As the South players performed their touchdown dance, the school bell rang.

"Had enough?" asked John.

"I think there's time for one more play," said William.

John's team punted the ball to William, who caught it in the end zone. He took the ball up the sideline. John dove at his feet, but William was too nimble for him and scored a touchdown.

The school bell rang.

"I didn't know William could run that fast," said Egypt.

"I thought you didn't like him anymore." Paris grinned.

"I didn't until I saw him in those tight green shorts, Philadelphia Eagles shirt, green socks, and green shoes," said Egypt. Egypt wanted to watch more of the game, but Paris didn't want to be late.

* * *

On the field, John jumped up and down like a little kid: "He stepped out of bounds." Then his cell phone buzzed. "Wait a moment."

While the rest of the students went to class, William approached John, who was talking on his cell surrounded by members of the LD03. John hung up his phone, placed it in the holder on his belt, and started looking around at everybody. Yet every time he made eye contact with anyone, they looked away. Each LD03 gang member knew the question.

"Who's going with me to pick up my girlfriend?" asked John.

Nobody said a word. John walked up to William. "Do you want to go?"

"Where?" asked William.

"To pick up my girlfriend," said John.

"What about your boys?"

"They're getting soft."

"I thought you didn't like me."

John smirked. "You remind me of me. So, you want to go or not?"

"Sure," replied William. "I don't want to go to boring first period anyway."

William got into John's white van, which was adorned with pictures of ice cream treats: popsicles, giant ice cream sandwiches, snow cones, push-ups, toasted almond bars, and fudge bars.

John drove out of the parking lot and stopped at McDonald's.

"Why are you stopping here?" asked William from the back seat.

"My girlfriend likes the hash browns and orange juice," replied John. "Would you like something?"

"Sure. Can I have two Egg McMuffins, a Southern-style country biscuit, a cinnamon melt, oatmeal, and a large orange juice?"

John ordered the food and pulled up to the drive-through window. The associate handed him two bags of food and beverages.

As John drove off to pick up his girlfriend, William asked, "How much do I owe you?"

"Don't worry about it," said John.

"I want to repay you."

"Help me sell some ice cream after school," said John as he pulled up to the park-and-ride lot of the transit station.

"Cool," said William.

"Just meet me at my van at the end of the day," said John.

He saw his girlfriend standing on the sidewalk. She raised her hand and waved. John pressed his foot on the brakes, and they let out a squeaking sound until the van stopped. She opened the door.

John's girlfriend hopped in and gave John a kiss. "Where's my food?" she asked.

He handed over the bag of food he had bought her. John put the van in drive and was about to pull out when his girlfriend scowled. "Just because you have a friend doesn't mean you can't feed me," she said. "I'll whoop your—"

Before John's girlfriend could finish her sentence, John pulled out a hash brown and handed it to her. She took a bite of it.

A text popped on William's Phone from Egypt. *Do you want to go to a fair with me on Saturday?*

John looked at William while his girlfriend finished her breakfast. "What's up?"

"That Egypt girl just asked me to go on a date," said William.

"Dog, answer her.... I think you can hit that."

William text back. *Yeah.*"

Chapter 6

As Egypt and Paris approached the gate of the Sweetest Day fair, they could see teenagers hanging upside down on roller coasters, spinning on the swashbucket, and kids stuffing their faces with hot dogs, French fries, pizza, cotton candy, fried Oreos, popcorn, chicken tenders, and hamburgers. Egypt turned up her nose.

"Why are you doing that?" asked Paris.

"The smell of carnival animals gets to me, but it has never stopped me from asking my father to take me to the fair," replied Egypt.

"I can't believe that your mother let you go on a date," said Paris as she snacked on some cookies.

Egypt stopped her car when a police officer blew his whistle at her. "Today is my birthday."

"What does that have to do with anything?" asked Paris.

"She said I could date when I turned sixteen."

"How did she react?"

"There was nothing she could say, and the fact you were coming along on a double date with me eased her mind."

"I love your mother," said Paris.

"That's because she thinks you're a good influence on me."

"Your mother is smart."

"Also, if she didn't have to prepare for a big case on Monday morning, I think she would have put up more resistance."

The police officer stopped traffic so that Egypt could turn. He then waved for Egypt to move. She floored the gas and flew by the officer, who gave her a mean glare. Egypt slowed down some and followed the parking attendant in a red vest into a parking spot.

"Now we just have to wait for William and John to text us," said Egypt as she turned off the car.

"Hopefully, they won't be too long," said Paris, still munching on her snack. "Why didn't you have a sweet sixteen birthday party?"

"You're looking at it," replied Egypt as she opened both hands wide.

"I don't understand."

"My mother gave me a choice between a car and a party."

"So, you chose . . . "

"My Volkswagen."

Egypt looked down at her phone. No text. "I hope they get here soon; I have to be home by 11 o'clock."

"What did your grandmother think about you going on a date?" asked Paris.

"She was the one that told my mother that it was time for me to date."

"Your grandmother is so sweet."

"I know."

Egypt turned and faced Paris. "Doesn't John have a girlfriend?"

"They broke up; it was all over Snapchat."

"Why did you agree to date a member of the LD03?" asked Egypt. "I thought you hated them."

Paris was silent for a moment. "I have my reasons, but I can't tell you right now."

A text popped up on Egypt's phone. *We're at the back gate.* "Let's go," said Egypt, as she and Paris exited the car.

While Egypt and Paris were walking toward the gate, Paris asked, "What changed your mind about William?"

"Because it's Sweetest Day," replied Egypt.

"What is that?" asked Paris, with a puzzled look on her face.

"Every third Saturday in October is Sweetest Day, a day for people who love each other."

"You and William are not lovers."

"Not yet," said Egypt with a devilish grin on her face.

"I still don't understand."

"My father use to take me to the fair every Sweetest Day, and we had the best time in the world. I love the rides, getting stuck on the Ferris wheel, and eating so much cotton candy that I got sick. My mother would be so mad, but I loved every minute of it. Since he couldn't be here, I thought, maybe, I could have a little of that fun with William. Is that silly?"

"Not really," said Paris.

As the girls approached the gate, William and John waved and jumped up and down, just inside the fence. The attendant scanned each girl's tickets on their phones, and they walked into the park. John and William were each holding roses in their hands. William gave his roses to Egypt, and she hugged him. John tried to give Paris his roses, but she snatched them out of his hand and threw them in a trash container.

Paris ran off toward the games section of the fair. John tried to catch her, but Paris's was a lot faster than John realized, and he had to run to catch her.

Egypt swung back and forth with the flowers in her hand, not sure what to think about Paris and John.

"That just leaves us," said William.

"I guess so," said Egypt.

"What do you want to do first? asked William.

"I'm not sure."

"How about getting something to eat?"

"Sure."

Egypt and William walked to the food stand that sold funnel cakes. After waiting in line for a few minutes, William ordered a funnel cake with sugar powder on it, along with two bottles of water. The couple sat down at a picnic table near the food stand. Egypt and William bowed their heads, as Egypt laid her roses down.

"Bless the food we are about to receive, "said Egypt. She pulled apart a piece of the cake and stuck it into William's mouth. Afterward, William put a piece of cake into Egypt's mouth. It didn't take long for the couple to finish it.

"Let's ride a roller coaster," said William.

"Sure," replied Egypt.

The couple stood in line for about thirty minutes before they got into a cart to go on the Southern Scream, the fastest roller coaster at the fair. As they were climbing up the first hill of the rollercoaster, they could see Paris and John arguing in front of a ticket counter.

"What that's about?" asked Egypt as the roller coaster car stopped.

"I don't know," said William as the coaster sped down the hill, and he started screaming. By the time the ride had ended, William's eyebrows were raised and his mouth stood half-open.

"Do you want to go on a slower ride?" asked Egypt.

William nodded.

"My father use to take me on the bumper cars," said Egypt. "What about them?"

William frowned.

"What's wrong?" asked Egypt.

"My father never took me to a fair in my life…."

"Why?"

He was too busy with the family business."

"Love, can I show you the ropes?"

William smiled and grabbed Egypt's hand as they approached the bumper cars. Egypt and William were able to get cars, and they rode around the track a few times before bumping into each other, smiling and laughing, while they were jerked forward and backward in their seats.

After getting off the ride, Egypt asked, "Can we play some games?"

"Sure," replied William

They approached the dart game, and William paid for three darts. He handed them to Egypt, who tried to hit the different colored balloons on a board, but the dart fell in the grass before it could hit the target.

William burst out laughing.

"That's not funny," said Egypt as she giggled.

"I'll help you," said William. He hugged Egypt from behind and grabbed her hand that was holding the darts. Together, they popped a pink and blue balloon, winning dolphin and panda bear stuffed animals.

As Egypt and William finished playing their game, Paris and John walked toward them. John had mud stains on his pants and Paris had straw sticking out of her curls.

"Love, are you okay?" asked Egypt.

"Yes," replied Paris.

Everybody was quiet for a moment. Then, John suggested, "We should go on the cave ride."

"I'll go," said Paris, "but John, don't touch me."

Egypt, Paris, William, and John walked to the cave ride. When it was their turn, Paris and John got into a small boat that had some water inside of it when they sat down. John tried to move close to Paris, but she moved to the other side of the boat as the attendant pulled the lever to release them. Paris and John disappeared into the cave.

Egypt put her prizes in a cubby next to the ride, and she and William stepped into a boat and slid next to each other. The attendant released the lever, and the couple rode into the cave with water splashing into the boat. William grabbed Egypt's hand and held it for a few minutes as they traded affectionate glances.

William pointed out several features of the caves that he had learned about from the Discovery Channel. William stretched out his arm and put it around Egypt's shoulder. The boat stopped at Mistletoe Point, a place where a piece of mistletoe hung over the top of the cave. William and Egypt turned to each other and locked lips. As they broke apart, saliva popped in the air and a rainbow formed in the liquid. They were motionless for a few moments until applause from the crowd broke their trance. Paris and John were waiting for them with their arms folded.

William got out first and helped Egypt onto the platform. After grabbing her stuff, Egypt and John joined Paris and John.

"Are y'all ready to go?" asked Paris, staring at John.

Egypt smiled. "Yes."

The group headed to the exit, and Egypt and William held hands. When they got to Egypt's car, Paris and John headed to the passenger's side. John tried to kiss Paris, but she pushed him away and got into the car. Egypt put both her arms around William and gave him a big kiss.

Egypt jumped into her Volkswagen. After the boys left, Egypt turned to Paris still gleaming. "What's up with you and John?"

"I can't tell you at the moment."

CHAPTER 7

Egypt couldn't believe she had to get Mr. G's room ready for the Ladies In Action (LIA) meeting. She had only attended two meetings, but she owed Paris a favor. When Egypt walked into the room, she almost fainted she saw the wasteland. Water bottles, textbooks, papers, notebooks, pens, pencils, candy wrappers, crumbs from Cheetos, and muffins were littered all over the desk in Mr. G's classroom. Book bags, clothes, and paper were splattered across the floor. Chairs were scattered around the room, out of place.

She thought, *How in the world will I get the room ready for the meeting that starts in fifteen minutes?* But she took a deep breath and sprang into action as Mr. G's pet mouse, Mickey, ran around his cage. Egypt stacked the books on the bookshelf in the back of the room, throwing the clothes in a cabinet, tossing the paper into the garbage. She brushed the crumbs into the dustpan, using a small broom that Mr. G kept under his sink, and tossed them away. Just as she finished, several girls knocked on the door, an Egypt let them in.

Jada walked into the class wearing a green jacket and carrying a book bag that she threw down into a seat. She placed her banana on the desk, holding her purse in her arms as she listened to music through AirPods in her ears. She sat down, pulled out some pages from her notebook, and began writing.

Susan skipped to her seat in a purple and white skirt. She crossed her legs, opened up a honey bun and started texting. Carmen walked to the back of the room, stroked her natural hair, and waved out of the window to her friend, who was eating breakfast in the courtyard. The girls had been chatting quietly but stopped what they were doing when Paris, the president, entered the room.

Egypt passed out the agenda, and Paris opened the meeting with a moment of meditation. Egypt closed her eyes as tight as she could and began to pray. *I can't understand why I can't find my father. Help me locate him, not only for the silly father-daughter dance, but also because a girl needs her daddy. I miss him and all of the fun games we used to play, such as ride the pony where I rode on my daddy's back. I miss jumping on his stomach as a little girl. Please help me find my daddy.*

Egypt heard giggles; she didn't realize that Paris had finished the moment of silence. Paris began the meeting by dictating the club's fundraising and service activities. Egypt daydreamed about the prayer porch at her old school, Saint Ignatius; they called it time-out at Eastside. At her old school, the sisters would often send students to the prayer porch when they needed time to reflect. Egypt spent more time at the prayer porch in the spring than usual; she had hit a student with a chair, Becky.

Becky was a student at Saint Ignatius who had been bullying Egypt all year; she had told Egypt several times that she didn't like brown people. One day she asked Egypt to show her the amulet of Bastet her father gave her, but Egypt refused. So Becky poured chocolate milk on Egypt. Before she knew it, Egypt had picked up a chair and she had hit Becky over the head with it. The principal let Egypt stay at the school for the rest of the year because Becky had been bullying her, but Egypt had to spend one hour a day at the prayer porch. At first, Egypt hated it, but after a while, she couldn't wait to be alone so that she could find peace.

The memories of her time at the prayer porch brought a peaceful calm over her until the door flew open. India burst into the meeting and scanned the room. When she spotted Egypt, India ran to the back of the room and sat next to her. The smell of India's sweat almost suffocated Egypt; it was like weed and musk. At that moment, the security guard walked into the classroom and looked at the girls. When he saw India in the back, he pointed a finger and abruptly gestured for her to come with him.

India began to get up, but Egypt stopped her.

"She's our newest member and she was just about to introduce herself," Egypt announced to the security guard.

Deciding to take advantage of Egypt's kindness and avoid Five-0's attempt to take her down, India stood up.

"Girls like me need your support," said India.

"I've been there," said Paris, but she shut up when India glanced over at her.

"Tell your story, sister," said Jada.

India continued. "My sister, my mother, and I have been living out of our car for the past six months."

The girls in the room gasped, and even the security guard felt guilty; he eased out of the room.

"It wasn't always this bad," said India.

"What happened?" asked Jada.

"My mother got sick."

"Was it cancer?"

India was quiet for a few moments. All of the young ladies in the room were on the edge of their seats until she spoke. "She's not been in her right mind for a while."

"Why didn't she go to the hospital?" asked Jada.

"We don't have health insurance."

"My mother is a psychologist," said Jada.

"We don't need any help," said India.

Paris jumped in. "Do you have a card?"

"Yes," replied Jada.

Jada pulled out a card from her purse and offered it to India. "Maybe you can take it and use it if you ever need it."

"OK," said India as she took the card from Jada and sat down.

Egypt whispered, "That was a great story. How did you make it up so fast?"

"Who said I made it up?" replied India.

Egypt was stunned; she couldn't believe anybody could live like that.

Paris got everybody's attention. "Our newest member has provided us with a lesson we won't forget for a long time."

As the LIA members stood in line for doughnuts, fruit, and juice, Egypt decided to walk over to India, who was looking at herself in a mirror.

"Your hair is so straight," said Egypt. "Did the Dominicans do it?"

"No," replied India. "I did it myself."

"Who braided your hair?" asked India.

"My mother's friend from the Bahamas," said Egypt.

"Did you know Egyptian women used to braid their hair to keep cool?" India, the human fact machine, said matter-of-factly.

"I didn't. How did you know that?"

"I read at the library while my sister and I wait for my mom to pick us up sometimes."

Egypt didn't think India was telling the truth, so she decided to change the subject. "Tell me about your father."

"I've never met him."

"Why not?" Egypt asked, trying to sound caring.

"He dumped my mother in high school; he said he wasn't her baby's daddy."

"You mean he's never claimed you?"

"Nope."

"Well, you don't seem very upset about it."

"I can't be angry at somebody I never met."

Egypt played with her amulet. "My father just left one day when I was nine, and I haven't seen him since."

"Do you know why?"

"Nope. I've been looking for him."

Suddenly, several girls screamed at the top of their lungs and ran behind Mr. G's desk. Egypt and India turned their heads toward the counter and saw a small mouse, the cause of the commotion.

Mr. G's pet mouse, Mickey, had gotten out of its cage and was running around the classroom. As Mickey ran toward India, she crawled onto the top of the science table and started throwing stuff at him. Egypt didn't move. Instead, she got down on her knees and picked up the little mouse. She held the small creature like her favorite baby doll, rubbing the top of its head, and then put it back in its cage, checking the lock three times to make sure it was secure. The LIA members applauded, and Mickey exercised on the wheel in the cage as if nothing had happened.

"Are there any more of them?" asked India.

"A whole family," insisted Paris.

"She's pulling your leg, love," said Egypt. "There's only Mickey, but he is part of Eastside. Some of the students have even knitted little vests for him."

Preparing to clean herself up after holding the mouse, Egypt waved for India to join her at the counter.

"Let's eat!"

"I'm not hungry," hollered India, who had finally gotten up the nerve to sit back down in her seat.

Egypt picked up a bottle of sanitizer, squeezed a handful of liquid into her hands, and rubbed her hands together.

Then Egypt brought a plate of grapes and sat back down next to India. "I can't believe you're not going to eat."

"I didn't get a chance to thank you for helping me out earlier," said India.

"No problem," said Egypt

"I can't afford to get suspended again. They would kick me out of school for good this time, and my mother would kill me."

"I haven't seen you at the debutante meetings lately," said Egypt.

"My mom needs my help at home, "said India with a sad look on her face. "Are you still panning to go to the debutante ball?"

"Yes, but I still can't find my father for the father-daughter dance."

"I think I can help you find your father."

Chapter 8

For the past few mornings, the sun had shone through the skylights of the cafeteria Eastside High School, blinding students trying to review for quizzes and finishing up the homework they should have done the night before. Yet today the cafeteria seemed dull; the windows sported freshly spray-painted letters that spelled out an expression. The LD03 gang had spent all night working on the project and waited in the halls to see the students' reactions. It wasn't until the administrators released the students from the gym into the cafeteria that the LD03 heard students burst out laughing. William and the other gang members ran into the cafeteria to investigate.

Girls and boys were rolling on the floor, giggling uncontrollably, but it didn't seem like it was because of the expression on the windows. William didn't understand and was concerned because this operation was supposed to get him off ice-cream duty. He had to find out why people weren't taking notice of his masterpiece. So he walked over to Egypt, who was ignoring the whoopla as she finished her homework; she had her head in her algebra book. She didn't get a chance to finish her teacher's assignment because she was too busy looking for clues about her father on social media sites.

He sat down next to her and asked why people were laughing, but Egypt kept solving her exponential equations with logarithms. William wrote her a note and slid it next to her. Egypt picked up the note and read it. She scribbled a response and handed it back to him; India's weave had fallen out and everybody was watching her stitch it back into her hair in the corner of the lunchroom.

William walked over to the lunch table where India was sitting on a circle seat and a crowd of students had gathered around her. She took some Peruvian hair and weaved it into her hair in a circular pattern. A friend of India placed a thread through a needle, tied a knot to secure the thread in place, and then handed the needle and thread to India. The girls in the crowd looked with their mouths wide open as India began weaving her hair, as if she was combing her hair in the mirror.

William couldn't believe that all his work had been wasted. William had to do something, so he walked back to Egypt.

Egypt looked up at him. "Love, what's wrong with you?"

"Nothing," said William.

A text popped on Egypt's phone. *Did you get to school safe?* Egypt texted a response. *Yes, mother. I'm finishing some homework. Send me a message when you leave school,* texted Mrs. James

OK, replied Egypt.

Egypt went back to work, feverishly trying to use the product rule of logarithms to complete the problems. William looked around the cafeteria and got the attention of the other LD03 members, who were waiting for his signal. He motioned to them to meet him in the middle of the cafeteria. The rest of the students were too busy enjoying the weaving demonstration to notice that the LD03 members were gathering, huddling together as tightly as possible, as William began to give them instructions.

He slipped out of the group and stood next to Egypt, who had just finished her last logarithm problem by using the identity base rule to obtain the solution. His presence surprised her; she had been concentrating so much on her homework that she hadn't noticed he was there.

She was about to ask him something when the LD03 members began to get loud. Then a gang member punched a student in the face while another jumped him from behind. Students started throwing biscuits, trays and chairs at the LD03 gang members. Principals and teachers showed up, but the students made a circle around the fight so they could not stop it. Egypt jumped into William's arms and held on to him as tightly as she could.

The security guards broke through. They picked up the gang members and toted them away, each one tucked under the arm of a security guard. The boys kicked and screamed all the way to the office.

"Is it over?" asked Egypt in a muffled voice, still holding on to William; her mouth was pressed against his red T-shirt.

"Yes," replied William, smiling.

Egypt lifted her head to catch her breath, but she started hyperventilating. She tried to speak, but William couldn't understand a word that was coming out of her mouth. Egypt pointed to her purse.

William grabbed the Louis Vuitton bag from the table and handed it to Egypt. She unzipped it, pulled out her inhaler, and took a couple of puffs as William rubbed her back.

"Thank you," Egypt said as she sat down. "For a moment, I thought you were my father; he used to stroke me like that when I had an attack."

"Do you need anything else?" asked William in a concerned voice.

"Some water," she replied, and pointed to her lunch bag.

William pulled out a water bottle, unscrewed the top, and put it up against Egypt's lips. She took a few sips. "Thank you."

"Are you OK?" asked William, not sure what to think.

"I'll be fine," said Egypt. "The fight made me nervous. That's the first fight I've ever seen in school."

"You're kidding."

"Nope," said Egypt as she took a few more puffs from her inhaler.

"Ready to go back to your old school?"

"No . . . I can't go back there."

The bell rang, which made Egypt jump. The altercation had left her shell-shocked. An administrator picked up a bullhorn and pressed the button to turn it on.

As the administrator barked orders, the students began to

ignore the hair-weaving demonstration. They got up from their tables, leaving their trays behind. Egypt began to put her books and notebook back into her book bag. She tried to throw her bag on her shoulder, but William stopped her and put it on his shoulder. The two began to walk to class, holding hands, when Egypt jerked away from him and ran back to the table to grab her purse.

Egypt walked back to William, who was waiting for her near the entrance of the lunchroom.

"I thought you didn't want to hold my hand," he said.

"No," said Egypt. "I forgot my purse."

All of a sudden, the students, including Egypt, stopped walking out of the cafeteria and looked up at the skylights, noticing the graffiti.

"Was that there yesterday?" asked Egypt.

"Nope," said William, who could hardly keep himself from revealing that he was responsible for the graffiti.

"Do you know who created it, love?"

William took a deep breath, filled with a deep sense of pride. "I did."

Egypt looked closely at the word: *Bastet*. She grabbed William by the shirt. "Who told you to write that?"

"I can't tell you."

Egypt glared at William, with a look that mothers use to scare their children, and William said in a chirp, "Baba."

"Say it louder," said Egypt as she shook William.

William cleared his throat. "Baba."

"Who's that?" asked Egypt.

For a moment William didn't say a word. "He's . . . the head of the LD03."

Egypt let go of William's jacket.

"Why does that phrase mean so much to you?"

With tears in her eyes, Egypt grabbed her amulet and cried, "This is Bastet that my father gave to me when I was nine."

Chapter 9

As beads of sweat rolled down Egypt's face, she thought that she should have skipped band practice to avoid the heat. It didn't help matters that her stomach was queasy from lunch: chicken so dry you could see the bone, mash potatoes with yellow sauce that students might have tested as the contents for a science fair project, and delicious hot bread. Yet Egypt stayed at attention, holding on to her clarinet as tight as she could.

Lumps of brown grass covered Egypt's white tennis shoes and the overgrown blades couldn't drown out the pungent smells of the dead grass that had accumulated because of extensive heat and rain. The freshmen of the band had marked the fields with lime, so it looked like a football field. However, it had rained so much that the lines were washed away, and the lime had fertilized the grass, which made it grow so fast that the custodian couldn't cut it fast enough.

Egypt and the rest of the band were waiting for the drum major to blow his whistle to start the routine. Just as they were about to start, the band came under attack; a barrage of rocks came flying from behind the band. Egypt, Paris, and the other clarinets took cover, running around the field to avoid the projectiles. Nobody got hit, but the percussion section couldn't help laughing at the girls.

"Love, do you think it's over?" Egypt asked.

"Yes," replied Paris.

After Egypt and Paris were sure the attack had ended, they walked back to position on the thirty-yard lines. Egypt growled, "Why are boys so stupid?" She wiped the sweat from her head and looked over at Paris. "It's hot out here."

"I said the same thing to myself," said Paris, looking up at Egypt.

After a few minutes, the drum major was able to get the sections back into formation. He blew the whistle, and the band started the routine, but some lines were crooked as they marched into fanfare position. The band played "Fanfare for the Common Man," but they sounded awful; the drummers were offbeat, the woodwind section was too high, and the brass section was too low. The drum major made the entire band run laps.

"I didn't know that I had to be an Olympic athlete to play in the band," said Egypt as she started running around the track with Paris.

"If I can do it," said Paris, "you should have no problem."

Egypt and Paris continued to jog around the track. "Love, you can move."

"My mother makes me work out on Saturdays at the gym."

"That's good," said Egypt.

"Yeah, but afterward we go get a stack of pancakes.

"Love, that defeats the purpose."

"I know, but I can't get enough of them."

When the girls finished their laps, they got back in line, but Egypt started huffing and wheezing, trying to catch her breath. She reached into her jeans pocket, pulled out her inhaler, and took a few puffs. The medicine worked; it relaxed the muscles in her lungs and cleared the passageways. Egypt felt fresh air flowing and she could breathe.

Egypt heard the blare of the drum major's whistle. She, along with the band, took off as one unit. Their lines were straight, the pinwheels moved like a bicycle wheel into the fanfare position, and their instruments snapped to play position. When they played the "Fanfare," the clarinets blew a sweet chorus, the brass section resonated the harmony, and percussion pushed the tempo.

When the band finished, the drum major stood on a stand, quiet for a few minutes; the members were in play position, too scared to move. Then he signaled to them to go to the ready position, and the band members' instruments rested by their sides. After a moment, he gave them a round of applause. The band members exhaled and broke into jubilance. The boys gave one another high-fives and the girls hugged one another. Egypt was thrilled to be part of a practice where they had received their first praise from the drum major.

As Egypt and Paris broke their embrace, they smiled at each other. The drum major blew the whistle to get everyone's attention again. The students ran as fast as they could back to their starting position. Before Egypt could get her instrument off the ground, a big rock hit the back of her head. She fell to the ground, the impact knocking her out.

Paris was the first to reach Egypt, but the rest of the band members also rushed to help her. They encircled her, limiting the amount of air that reached her. Paris pushed them back as she knelt down next to Egypt.

"Are you OK?" asked Paris as Egypt began to wake up.

Egypt looked dazed. "What happened?"

"A rock hit you in the head," said Paris, and the other band members watched her as she spoke every word.

"It was huge," said a band member.

Paris turned around and hollered at him, "Imbecile, shut up!"

Egypt sat up, and Paris handed her some water. She took a few slips and smiled.

"If I knew that band practice was this rough, I would've joined the football team," said Egypt.

The band laughed. Paris pulled Egypt to her feet. There was red clay on her knees and grass blades sticking to her T-shirt. Paris picked off the grass and dusted off Egypt's amulet.

"I thought Bastet was supposed to protect you," said Paris.

"Against spells, not stupid boys," said Egypt.

Before Paris could ask more questions, the girls saw security dragging members of the LD03 gang and William to the drum major. Egypt and Paris looked at each other but didn't say a word; they knew it was about the rock. After a few minutes, the drum major signaled to Egypt to come to her. She walked over to the security guard and told them what had happened. She then walked back to her space in front of Paris.

"What happened?" asked Paris.

"Security caught the LD03 throwing rocks," said Egypt.

"William too?"

Egypt turned around. "I don't think so."

"Why?"

"Paris, he wouldn't hurt somebody he loves."

"How do you know that's true?"

"He kissed me this morning when he walked me to class," said Egypt.

"Did he say it?"

Egypt frowned. 'No."

"It isn't so until he says it."

Chapter 10

Egypt had to stay after band practice so the football trainer could make sure she didn't have a concussion. After he cleared her, she walked down the stairs that led from the field to the parking lot. Halfway down, she stopped. The drum section was marching around the cars had blocked in the activity bus. The bus driver stuck his head out of the window and hollered at them to get out of the way, but they were laughing so hard they didn't even hear him.

Egypt started to run for her car, but the drum major grabbed her by the shirt and pointed to the band room door. "Put up your instrument."

"O.K." sighed Egypt.

She flew into the band room, almost knocking down the band

director on the way. She opened her locker in a flash, threw her clarinet case inside, and ran out.

Now, as Egypt ran from the school building toward her car, she kept thinking about what the drummers might have done to her Volkswagen Bug. If it had suffered a single scratch, her mother would never let her drive it again. Egypt couldn't get through the crowd of people surrounding her car, giggling at what somebody was saying. She jumped up and down but couldn't see her car.

Egypt got down on her hands and knees and crawled between the band members' legs, enduring the pebbles scraping against her legs. When she reached the middle of the circle, she found India leaning on the hood of the car. Egypt stood up and tapped her on the shoulder.

"Please do not lean on my vehicle," said Egypt as India jumped up from the hood.

"I could lean on your face," said India as the crowd encouraged Egypt and India to engage in a confrontation.

While the other students continued to egg on Egypt and India, they didn't notice that the drum major was making a path to them through the crowd, pushing the kids aside. Once he reached them, he sat both of them on the curb and ordered the rest of the band to leave. The drummers marched back toward the field for more practice. The drum major turned toward the girls, who were still glaring at each other.

"I'm not sure what the problem is," said the drum major, "but I'm not putting up with this crap on my watch."

Egypt and India tried to get a word in, but he began lecturing them. The girls would rather have gotten a beating than hear another sermon.

"You girls will have to learn to get along," the drum major finished. "So, Egypt, you will take India home."

"She can't ride in my—" started Egypt.

"Be quiet!" hollered the drum major before she could finish. "If India can't ride with you, your mother will be getting a call."

"Who's going to keep us from killing each other?" asked India.

"Y'all will have to figure that out," replied the drum major as he walked back to the school.

Egypt and India got into the Volkswagen Bug and sped out of the parking lot. They headed up the street and had been quiet for a few minutes when India asked Egypt if they could stop to get something to eat.

Egypt didn't want to stop, but she thought that if she was nice to India, her mother wouldn't get called. So they pulled into the parking lot and went inside a restaurant.

India got in line. "Are you going to order something?"

"No," answered Egypt. "My supper is waiting for me at home."

"Well, my mother has to work this evening; she got a new job."

"What does she do?"

"She's an entertainer," said India as the clerk tried to get her attention. "She uses a lot of the drill team girls in her performances."

"Do you think I could be one of her performers?"

India smiled sarcastically. "You don't have enough rhythm."

After a few minutes, India, eating French fries out of a bag, came over to the booth where Egypt was sitting. "Can you drop me at the train station?"

"Sure," replied Egypt as the girls left the restaurant. They got into the car, and Egypt backed out of the parking space. She floored the accelerator.

"Watch out for the child!" screamed India.

Egypt slammed on the breaks. The child's mother ran out behind the car and picked up her crying child. Egypt couldn't move; she was shaking all over. India caressed her shoulders. "Nobody got hurt," she said.

"I couldn't live with myself if I had hit that little girl," said Egypt.

"You didn't," said India. "So, next time, slow down when you're in a parking lot. Now, drive me to the train station."

"OK," said Egypt as she took out her inhaler and took a few puffs. She drove below the speed limit to the station.

"I'm sorry about giving you a hard time at the school," said India. "I have a reputation to uphold."

"No problem."

"Plus, I owe you one for helping me get away for Five-0."

"You sure do."

"If you want to find your father for the debutante ball, hang out at the Gallery," said India as she got out of the car and walked to the train station.

Chapter 11

The football coach began the pep rally by bragging and hollering, "We're going to clobber Westside High School," but the LD03 gang members began to pop balloons as he tried to get the crowd hyped. The principal went into the stands and proceeded to drag several members of the gang out of the gym. After introducing his players, the coach gave the microphone to the drum major. He blew the whistle, the lights dimmed, and the drummer brought out a table with a person lying down on it.

The shrill of the drum major's whistle brought to life the person lying on the table; it was William, dressed like a dragon. He started a dance routine, which fired up the crowd, and the students started stomping on the bleachers and screaming at the top of their lungs. When the music ended, the dragon descended onto the platform, and the band members took William out of the gymnasium. The crowd gave William a standing ovation, and it took several minutes before they calmed down.

Next, the cheerleaders got the crowd quiet and huddled in the middle of the gym. They shook their pom-poms and kicked their legs high in the air, conducting a cheer that the school joined in. At the end of the performance, several cheerleaders backflipped the length of the gym. Suddenly, India jumped out of the eleventh-grade section and walked across the floor to the ninth-grade section.

"Where is she going?" asked Egypt as she sat down on the gym bleachers.

"To her right class," said Paris as she crossed her leg

"What do you mean, love?"

"She's in a ninth-grade home room."

"How?" whispered Egypt into Paris's ear.

"India fails all her classes."

"Paris, is she that dumb?"

"No, she just misses school a lot."

"Why?"

"She has to take care of her sister."

A roar came from the freshmen section as India shook her breasts in a sexual manner. The freshmen boys, who up to that point had not been paying attention, jumped in front of her and started throwing dollars, making it rain with money. The senior guys sprinted across the gym to see the show. The female teachers sprang into action, diving into the melee and pulling India out of the crowd. Her shirt was torn, the sleeves hanging off her arms. The teacher led her into the principal's office.

Finally, the bell rang, and the students filed out of the gym. Egypt and Paris stood at the top of the bleachers, watching the students leave. The band played their fight song, and the cheerleaders continued to cheer as people left.

"I can't believe India did that," said Egypt as she walked down the gym bleachers with Paris, watching the crowd file out of the gym. "What type of dancing was that?"

"Shake dancing," said Paris as they stepped onto the gym floor and walked toward the lobby. "It means just move something."

"Who taught her how to dance like that?" asked Egypt.

"Her mother," said Paris. "She used to be an exotic dancer."

Egypt and Paris continued to walk toward the entrance of the gym. "How long has India been dancing?"

"Since elementary school," replied Paris. "She taught us a few moves in the bathroom."

"Love, do you know how to shake dance?"

"A little." Paris smiled.

"Do you think you could teach me?" asked Egypt, looking embarrassed.

"Why?"

"I can't dance," said Egypt as the girls walked into the concession area, where the engineering club was selling snacks.

"Maybe, but right now I want some food," said Paris.

Students were crowded around the stand; Paris and Egypt couldn't even see what the club was selling. Finally, they got to the front of the line. They surveyed the candy, popcorn, pizza, hotdogs, drinks, and goodies as the other students prompted them to hurry up and make a selection.

Egypt started to remind Paris about her diet, but Paris volunteered to pay first, and Egypt was too hungry to argue with her. They walked out of the concession area with pizza and soda. While they walked past the main office, they saw a woman hollering at the principal.

"Who's that?" asked Egypt, staring at the woman.

"It's not nice to stare," replied Paris as she grabbed Egypt and pulled her to the front of the building. "That's India's mom."

"Oh," said Egypt. A young man opened the door for the girls. They sat on the benches in front of the high school and finished their snacks. "She sure got here fast."

"India's mother helps the LD03 recruit girls when she is not sick," said Paris.

"What do you mean?"

Paris handed Egypt a modeling flyer that was on the ground in front of them.

"I still don't understand."

"The LD03 tricks high school girls into thinking they will be models, but they want them to give private dances for men."

"How do you know?" asked Egypt.

"I've danced before, at the Gallery."

Egypt almost choked. "When?"

"As a freshman. Men pay big bucks to see young girls dance."

"India said my father hangs out at the Gallery, the best teen club on the eastside of Atlanta, GA."

"I might have seen him there."

"How do you know how he looks?" asked Egypt as she put her palm on Paris's cheek and turned it so that Paris's face was directly in front of her.

"His picture was on your phone," said Paris.

"Oh," said Egypt.

Chapter 12

The line to get into Memorial Stadium in Stone Mountain wrapped around the building; everybody wanted to see the game of the year between Eastside and Douglass High School on Halloween. The administrators were not taking any chances this year; several students went home with war wounds after last year's contest. So everybody had to be scanned. Purses were frisked, and males had to empty their pockets of wallets, keys, and cell phones.

The stands were filled, and people were everywhere, looking like ants in an anthill.

The cheerleaders unrolled the banner that displayed an Eastside Eagle with a Douglass Astro in its beak, the sight of which brought a roar from the Eagles. Then, as they stood the sign up, the wind ripped it apart. The girls scrambled to grab the pieces of the banner as the band started playing the fight song and the football team charged onto the field.

The captains of the football teams walked to the middle of the field to flip the coin, as the drums reverberated throughout Memorial Stadium.

The Eastside Eagles were hosting Douglass, the number one ranked team in the state. The Astros star running back, Jeremiah Jones wanted to pay back Eastside. They had knocked the Astros out of the playoffs last year. The referee tossed the coin into the air, and landed on heads. Eastside got the ball first.

The teams huddled up on the field. Stephen dropped back into the end zone, awaiting the kick from Jeremiah Jones. Jeremiah walked back a few feet behind the forty-yard line, while a teammate held the ball with a finger to keep the wind from knocking it over. He looked over to the referee, who blew his whistle. Jeremiah sprinted toward the ball and kicked it, which sent the ball high into the air. As Stephen waited for gravity to bring the ball down, he wondered if India would go out with him if he scored a touchdown. He snapped back to the game as he caught the ball. Stephen sprinted toward the other end zone while Jeremiah ran down the field, knocking Eastside players out of the way.

At about the twenty-yard line, Stephen and Jeremiah collided. Jeremiah latched onto Stephen's arm, and he dragged the star player down the field. Around the fifty-yard line, he let go and fell face-first into the middle of the field. Stephen raced to the end zone with the crowd screaming and the band playing a funky tune. As Eastside cheered, the trainers from Douglass raced to the field to help Jeremiah, but he pushed them aside and stomped back to the sideline.

The crowd became so loud that the referees had to stop the game; they walked over to Eastside's coach and told him that his team was going to get a penalty for noise. The coach turned to the fans and tried to get them to shut up, but when the crowd saw the limos at the gate behind the track, they couldn't control themselves. The head official blew his whistle and threw a yellow flag on the field; the team was penalized for unsportsmanlike conduct. The coach threw his headset against the ground, sending pieces of the device into the fence behind the home team's bench.

"I wonder what's the holdup," said Egypt from the back seat of the limo for the homecoming court.

It's not halftime yet," said Paris, sitting next to Egypt. "Security will let us in when it's time."

"I've never seen this many people before in my life," commented Egypt as she pushed in a hairpin that was sticking out of her hairpiece.

"Today isn't that crowded," said Paris. "Wait until we play Westside."

Paris reached into her purse and pull out a small pouch.

"Love, what's that?"

She handed it to Egypt. "It's your safety kit."

"Where did you get this from?"

"The girls at my sister's college are given them so they won't get pregnant or get a disease on dates."

Egypt handed it back to Paris and spoke. "I don't want it."

"It's better to be safe than pregnant," said Paris as she handed the black pouch back to Egypt again.

"I won't have to worry about that."

"Why?"

"William has not been around for the entire week," said Egypt as she took the pouch and opened it up. Inside, there were two condoms and a tube of lubricant.

"Why do I need lubricant?" asked Egypt.

"If you don't use it, sex can be painful."

"Love, is there something you need to tell me?" asked Egypt as she put the kit in her purse.

"I do," said Paris. "But not tonight. "I'm not saying that something is going to happen, but you always need to be prepared."

About this time the limousine driver slowly entered the gate.

"I'm glad we're moving," said Egypt, putting a napkin and a paper towel between her lips to remove access lipstick.

The limos crept around the track toward the overflowing crowd. The percussion section stood up, and the section leader led into a drum cadence, looking like a marine unit; they wouldn't dare miss a beat. The students in the stands screamed at the top of their lungs. As the vehicles got in front of the fans, they stopped. The queens got out of the cars and lined up on the pavement.

"Why are the students screaming?" asked Egypt as she stepped out of the limo and onto the track.

"The crowd goes crazy when the queens arrive," replied Paris as she waved to the crowd, along with the other queens.

Egypt had her braids in a bun with her amulet of Bastet necklace around her neck. The brilliance of the diamonds in her dress reflected white light throughout the crowd, almost blinding some spectators. Yet the split in her dress brought oohs and aahs from the crowd as she put her hands on her hips.

The queens walked through the open gate of the football field and stood in the end zone as the official blew the whistle for halftime. The football players ran toward the locker rooms.

As the young ladies approached the center of the field, fans cried out the name of their choice for homecoming queen. The court formed a semicircle facing the crowd, which became quiet when they came to a stop. The PA announced the ninth and tenth grade queens; the crowd clapped politely. As the announcer began announcing the eleventh-grade court, Egypt grabbed Paris's hand and closed her eyes. She was praying so hard she never heard her name called as the eleventh-grade queen; the other girls mobbed her with hugs.

As the girls broke their huddle, she could hear the crowd murmuring in confusion. Then she saw a motorcycle riding around the track. Egypt could not see the person, but the rider carried roses. The rider entered the field through a gate and parked the bike. When he pulled off his helmet, Egypt couldn't believe it was William. He walked up to Egypt, gave her the flowers and kissed her. William picked her up and put her on his motorcycle. He got on and she grabbed him around his waist. They drove out of the stadium with the crowd cheering.

Chapter 13

A neon sign, "The Gallery," shone over the door. Kids stood on a red carpet, and the bouncers were not allowing them into the club until the queens arrived. A section had been roped off with a steel stand, leather ropes, and a VIP sign placed on top of it. The windows were painted over so that nobody could see inside, even though the music kept rattling them.

The kids started cheering as a limousine pulled up in front of the door of the club. Two security guards, both the size of refrigerators, pushed the crowd farther down the sidewalk to clear the entrance. After the way was opened, the guards walked to the car, opened the doors, and escorted the queens into the homecoming party.

The security guards started allowing the teenagers in line into the club after all the queens were inside. They had given everybody who had arrived before 10:30 p.m. tickets so that they could get in free. The line was reduced to a few students when several cars pulled into the parking lot. One of the security guards pulled out his radio and called for backup as members of the LD03 walked to the entrance.

Police cars came from everywhere, blocking the LD03 pathway to the nightclub. They ordered the boys to lay face down on the cement. John and his boys followed the officers' orders. A bald police officer, sucking on a lollipop and wearing silver sunglasses, walked to John. He kicked his tennis shoes.

John jumped to his feet. "We haven't done anything wrong."

"You boys going to have to leave," said the officer.

"Why?" asked John.

"You can't go into the club with those jeans on," said the officer pointing to the sign hanging on the side of the ticket window: *"NO JEANS ALLOWED."*

John looked at the sign and cursed under his breath. "Let's go." The LD03 gang members walked to their cars and sped out of the parking lot—the sides of their vehicles illuminated with fluorescent lights.

As the LD03 left, William rode up to the club with Egypt on the back of his motorcycle. She had ditched her dress for a black leather outfit. They dismounted and pulled off their helmets.

The bald police officer had almost gotten into his police cruiser but stopped when he saw the couple walking toward the club. "How can I help you?" he asked.

William put his arm around the officer's shoulders like they were the best of buddies. "We came to celebrate," said William.

William could feel the officer stare at him through his sunglasses; he pulled his arm from around the officer and walked to Egypt. She grabbed William around the waist and hugged him as tight as she could.

"That's very touching," said the officer as he instructed the other officers to arrest William.

Egypt stepped in front of William, preventing the officers from putting on the handcuffs. She looked hard at the officer in charge. "Is that you, Uncle Terry?" asked Egypt.

The officer pulled off his sunglasses. "Egypt?" said Officer Terry, surprised to see his niece at the nightclub. "I don't think your father would like for you to be with a boy like this."

"He left us, remember?" said Egypt. "Plus, William and I are celebrating my coronation as Queen Eleventh Grade."

"Congratulations!" said Officer Terry, picking her up and turning her around. "You're my favorite niece."

"I'm your only niece." Egypt smiled as the officer put her down on the sidewalk.

"That's true," said her uncle.

"Can you do me a favor?" asked Egypt in a little-girl voice.

"Yes, but I know I'm not going to like it," mumbled Officer Terry.

"Can you tell me where my father is?"

"Why?"

"I need him for the father-daughter dance at my debutante ball," said Egypt.

"Y'all can go into the club because you know I can't do that," Officer Terry directed the security guards to let Egypt and William into the Gallery.

Some teenagers were on the dance floor, while other students were sitting at cocktail tables eating chicken wings and French fries and drinking sodas. As soon as Egypt and William entered, Egypt saw Paris heading to the bathroom. She walked toward her.

"Where are you going?" asked William.

"I need to talk to Paris," said Egypt as she left William standing near the bar.

John approached William. "Where's your girl?"

"She's with Paris," said William. "How did you get in?"

"India let us in the back door."

"I wish she would hurry up," said William.

"Egypt has whipped you."

"You don't know what you're talking about."

"If you were swol like me, you wouldn't be having these problems," said John.

"Stop jumping to conclusions," said William. "I let her have some slack on her leash, but she is my lightweight."

"It seems to me that she has broken the chain."

"John, if you take my girl, I'm not going to take it personally because she was never mine."

India came over and hugged William, but he jumped back, "Don't bother me."

"Aw shucks!" said India. "I should get the boys outside who just finished fighting to take care of you."

"What happened?" asked John excitedly.

"They were young boys, but they were big," said India. "They just bucked; they were fighting like they were in a no-holds bar."

"Who was fighting?" asked Egypt as she and Paris joined William, India, and John standing around the bar.

"These boys who got caught freakin'," said India.

"What's that?" said Egypt.

India put her hand over her mouth. "I keep forgetting that you are so young," said India, sticking out her tongue ring so that everybody could see.

That caught Egypt's eye. "Was it painful?" asked Egypt.

"Not as painful as the way girls hurt your feelings," said India.

Paris glanced over at John. "Boys hurt your heart."

"You don't have to tell our business," said John as he frowned.

Paris almost jumped at John, but India held her back because she knew that he had deflowered her in ninth grade. "Just chill," said India.

"Don't be like that," said John.

"You said that you loved me," cried Paris

John looked down at the floor. "It was a joke."

"Not to me," hollered Paris, who had gotten the attention of the entire club; the music was no longer bumping, kids had stopped dancing, and everyone gathered around the couple.

"Rejection breeds hatred," said Paris.

"Your nagging is starting to bother me," said John.

"Tell little man to shut up," said Paris, who brought oohs and aahs from the crowd.

"You need to stop talking," said John.

"I'll stop when I'm finished with my conversation," said Paris.

John started to get mad; the crowd seemed to be turning on him. "I should pop your behind!"

"Are you threatening me in front of all these people?" asked Paris.

"I'm straight," said John. "Why are you acting like you want to fight me?"

"I should beat you down," cried Paris with water in her eyes.

"Come on, let's go," said John, daring her to charge him.

Egypt, Paris, William, and the crowd looked at Paris, waiting for her to attack.

"Nobody is scared of this punk," said Paris. "Ugly boy! Why did you play me?"

Before John could answer, a voice from the crowd made a suggestion. "Somebody should hit that man for shorty."

Then another voice screamed, "Choke him!"

"Dude, tame that," said a member from the LD03 as Egypt tried to run to help her friend, but William pulled her back into the crowd.

"I can't fight, but I can fight back," said Paris as she walked toward John, who tried to walk away, but the crowd pushed him back into the circle.

"Stop playing," said John, swatting Paris's hands away as she pushed him.

"I'm for real," said Paris, chasing John.

"Leave me alone," said John. "This girl is stupid."

Egypt broke William's grip and ran to Paris's side. "Don't talk to my friend like that."

"That's sad how it went down," said John.

"I didn't deserve to be treated like that," said Paris as she held on to Egypt, crying.

The crowd started grabbing their noses and running toward the exit; somebody had farted.

"India stank," said William.

John and the LD03 took the opportunity to sneak out of the club.

Egypt and Paris hugged each other in the middle of the dance floor for a few minutes. Then William extended his hand to Egypt. "We need to go celebrate," he said.

"Love, are you OK?" asked Egypt.

"Yes," Paris replied. "It's time for you to enjoy your night."

"What are you going to do?" asked Egypt.

"I need to talk to your uncle Terry about something."

William took Egypt to a private room that was used for special parties. There were towels on the bed in the shape of a dolphin, Egypt's favorite animal, which reminded her of the last cruise trip she had taken with her mother. A mirror hung over the bed. A candle burned on a nightstand with the fresh scent of jasmine, and the covers were pulled back.

Egypt turned around, and William kissed her. Before she knew it, William had taken off her clothes. She fell on the bed, and William was on top of her so fast that she didn't have time to relax and warm up, use the lubricant Paris had given her in the limo.

"What are you doing?" shouted Egypt, as her eyelids tightened and grabbed the sheets as hard as could when William penetrated her. As William reached his climax, Egypt thought about what Paris told her about her first sexual experience in ninth grade: *Teenage boys just want to hit it.* That's why she dates men.

William and Egypt lay on the bed for a few minutes. Then William rolled over and put on Egypt's panties.

"Love, what are you doing?" asked Egypt.

"I'm trying them on," replied William.

Egypt wrestled her underwear away from him. William

thought Egypt was playing until she turned into her mother and gave him the death stare.

William stopped laughing. "I guess you are ready to go," he said.

"Yeah," said Egypt as she began to dress herself.

As Egypt and William came out of the room, she saw her father going into another room with Jada from LIA. Egypt ran to the door and banged on it for five minutes. Finally, the ninth grader came to the door. Egypt pushed her aside and ran into the room. Men were smoking cigars, sipping on cocktails, and enjoying girls from Eastside High School, dancing on a stage with almost no clothes on. Egypt looked for her father, but she didn't see him. Egypt walked back to the door and asked Jada, "Where is the man you were with?"

"I don't know what you are talking about," she said without looking Egypt in the eye.

Chapter 14

The town was like a ghost town, but lost spirits had gathered for a meal. Men huddled around an old steel drum with flames shooting out of it, rubbing their hands together, trying to transfer heat from the fire to their cold bodies. As they huddled, drivers sped by their tent city, a center the church provided to help the homeless. And God had sent angels from Eastside High School to help the homeless, the LIA.

The makeshift homeless shelter provided a place where men could take a bath, get a hot meal, and obtain medical care. As they waited for assistance, the men gossiped, argued, and prayed to God. If it weren't for the time of day and the sleeping bags along the wall, most people would think a church was having a revival meeting because of the huge tent the church had erected to serve the men food.

Moreover, Egypt couldn't believe that Mr. G. made them ride the rapid rail system to downtown Atlanta; she had never ridden mass transit before, and the riders made her nervous. To make matters worse, they had to walk to the shelter from the station in the cold. As they walked the winds swirled around the buildings, whipping students like circus animals as they crossed the street carrying plastic bags filled with toiletries collected from the students at Eastside for LIA's annual homeless campaign.

For a moment Mr. G. and the rest of the class stood on the corner of Peachtree Street and Juniper; Mr. G was lost. Then everybody started following Egypt; she had pulled out her phone and used her GPS to find the address of the Peachtree Pine Homeless Shelter, the largest in the Southeast

When Egypt reached the corner of Pine and Juniper, she had entered another world; hundreds of men were scattered in lots where people were tending to the wounded; doctors were treating patients, college students were handing out pamphlets, and women were serving hot meals. Egypt and her class were assigned to help with food.

After only a few minutes of serving, Egypt started feeling dizzy. She tried to keep her balance by grabbing onto Paris, who was standing next to her. But before she knew it, Egypt had fallen into Paris's arms. Paris lowered her to the ground, placing Egypt's head on a book bag.

A doctor who had been treating the homeless came to Egypt's side, while the rest of the volunteer students from Eastside gathered at her feet. The doctor placed some smelling salts under her nose as friends watched for signs of life. To everyone's relief, her eyes began to open as she regained consciousness. She tried to speak, but no sound came out. The doctor gave her a sip of water.

"What happened?" asked Egypt.

"You fainted," replied the doctor.

"How did that happen?"

"I'm not sure, but I think you're going to be fine," said the doctor.

Egypt and Paris sat down on the ground for a few minutes as the other students continued to serve the food. Egypt took a few more sips of water. She looked into her best friend's eyes and started crying. Paris gave her a long hug. Finally, Egypt wiped her eyes and let go of Paris.

"Do you want to talk about it?" asked Paris.

Egypt tried to speak, but only gibberish came out, unrecognizable words that sounded like a new language. Paris looked at Egypt, confused.

"I think we need to go inside," said Paris.

"Where?" asked Egypt.

"To the shelter," said Paris, pointing to the brown, two-story building, where women and children were being taken care of.

"Sure, I would like to get out of the cold for a few minutes."

One of the male volunteers, carrying a case of water, escorted the girls to the building, while the other volunteers from the LIA.

As soon as they walked into the building, a few of the women in the room woke up and a woman screamed, "That's what you want, a man with a fudge complexion."

The male volunteer blushed. After the young man left, the women settled down. Women and children could sleep in the building, but men were not allowed for safety reasons. Paris found some chairs where Egypt could rest while the volunteers served the women and children food in a buffet-style breakfast. Paris got Egypt some tea and sat down next to her.

"Shouldn't we help them serve?" asked Egypt.

"Sure," replied Paris. "But you need to rest first."

"Thanks. I'm still hurting from last night."

"What happened?"

"Love, I didn't know that sex would hurt that much."

"Did you use the kit?"

"I didn't have time," said Egypt.

"What do you mean?" asked Paris.

"We started doing it so fast that before I knew it, William had come."

"Inside of you?"

Egypt nodded her head.

"Do you know why I gave you the kit?"

"No," replied Egypt. "Was it because of John?"

"That's only part of the story. He not only deflowered me, but he also convinced me to become a dancer for the LD03."

"Like the girls last night."

"What are you talking about?"

"Last night I saw my father go into a room at the Gallery, and all of these girls who were dancing were from the LIA."

"Did you talk to him?"

"When I finally got into the room, he had disappeared."

"That's too bad," said Paris with a sad look on her face.

"What's wrong?" asked Egypt.

"Was Jada there?"

"Yes."

"Nothing has changed. Ninth graders are still dancing for men."

"How long has this been going on?"

"Since before I came to Eastside High School."

"That long?"

"Yup," said Paris. "After I had sex with John, I went crazy. I thought I was in love, and I did what he asked me to do."

"That dog," said Egypt.

"So, he asked me to dance at the Gallery."

"Like the girls I saw last night."

"Yeah," said Paris. "I thought we were making progress with the LIA."

"What do you mean?"

"Well, the LIA was started as a support group for girls like me and Jada, who have been exploited by men."

"Did you get paid as a dancer?"

"Yes."

"At least you made some money."

"That's what they want you to think, but it's like a drug."

"How so?" asked Egypt, confused.

"Once you get a little money and expensive gifts from men, it's never enough."

"How did you get out?"

"I got pregnant," replied Paris.

"You had an abortion?" whispered Egypt.

"No, I gave the baby up for adoption after attending a charter school for girls who are pregnant in North Carolina."

"How long were you there?"

"Until I had the baby."

"So that's why you were at the summer retreat in Charlotte when I met you."

"We both needed the mental break from school last year." Paris laughed.

"I know! That's right."

"There's one more thing."

"What?" asked Egypt.

"I've danced for your father."

"Why didn't you tell me that before?"

"I didn't know until I saw him in the background picture on your phone."

"That was weeks ago."

"I just didn't know how to tell you."

CHAPTER 15

Egypt was failing all her classes, but she didn't know how to tell her mother, as they drove to school for parent-teacher conferences while her nine-year-old cousin, Sagmus, sat in the back seat of the car playing a game on her phone. Egypt had been an honor student at private school, so Mrs. James assumed that nothing had changed. While they sat in traffic waiting to enter the school's parking lot, Egypt used her nervous energy to text Paris, asking her what she should do about William.

"How did you do on your progress report?" asked Egypt's mother.

Egypt acted like she didn't hear her and kept texting.

Mrs. James grabbed the phone from Egypt's hand. "Progress report?"

"Oh," said Egypt, "they had a problem printing my report. Something about my student number . . ."

"Well, I'll get one when I talk to Mr. G," said Mrs. James as traffic started to move. "How did Paris do?"

"I think she got all As."

"That's the kind of student I want you to hang around with," said Mrs. James as she turned her Volvo into the parking lot and parked in the "Teacher of the Year" space.

"Mom," said Egypt in an annoying, teenage voice, "you can't park here."

"Watch me," snapped her mother. "My taxes paid for this school!"

Egypt didn't respond. She just sat next to her mother for a moment before she sighed and said, "Why do we have to be here?"

Egypt's mother turned off the car and looked at Egypt. "I haven't had the chance to meet your teachers this year. I want to know who is teaching my child."

"They are just as nice as my teachers were last year, even nicer."

"Let's go so I can find out."

Egypt, Sagmus, and her mom walked toward the entrance of the school while the teachers were in the cafeteria, trying to grab something to eat. The PTA had provided hot wings, pizza, turkey subs, and soft drinks. Mr. G sat down with the other teachers from the science department and complained about the new furlough days for teachers as he stuffed cheese pizza and wings in his mouth and gulped down a can of soda.

The principal joined Mr. G to talk about the Science Olympiad; the school had won several state championships and even one national title. The principal had mounted lights on the ceiling that illuminated the banners to help inspire his students to keep the tradition alive. The principal wanted an update on the preparation for this year's competition, and Mr. G assured him that everything was on track as he rushed off to his first conference.

Egypt and her mother marched down the hall, stepping over dust piles filled with pencils and balled-up pieces of paper.

"Can I go to the bathroom?" asked Egypt.

"Hurry up," said Egypt's mother. "I don't want to miss my conference time." Sagmus leaned against the wall next to the bathroom. "Do you have to go to the restroom?" Mrs. James asked Sagmus.

"No, ma'am."

Egypt quickly used the comfort station, and when she, Mrs. James, and Sagmus approached Mr. G's room, they could see William sitting at a desk talking to him. They stood at the door waiting for them to finish.

"I thought that Mr. G hated William," said Mrs. James.

"They have a love-hate relationship," said Egypt.

William sat in a chair in front of Mr. G. They were discussing his grade report. William pointed to a missing assignment as his diamond earring sparkled across the room. He had a strained look on his face.

"William, I have a conference," said Mr. G. He could see Mrs. James steaming, mad that William was taking up her conference time.

"I'll talk to you later," said William to Mr. G as he walked toward Egypt and her mother.

"Love, did you have a rough night?" asked Egypt with a look of concern.

"I had to work at the Gallery last night, but I'm not the one they call 'Sleepy,'" William said as he left the room.

Mrs. James took her eyes off William and stared at Egypt, as Sagmus took a seat in the back of the room next to a skeleton model. "Why are people calling you that?" asked Mrs. James.

"I don't know what they're talking about," lied Egypt.

"I think I can explain," interrupted Mr. G, who then motioned for Egypt and her mother to sit in the chairs in front of his desk.

Mrs. James sat, but Egypt stood next to her chair.

"Do you want to sit?" asked Mr. G.

"She's practicing," commented her mother with her legs crossed.

"I don't understand," said Mr. G with a puzzled look.

"When I get through with Egypt, she's not going to be able to sit," said Mrs. James.

"Do I need to leave?"

"I'll take care of Egypt when I get home."

"First, I would like to apologize for William being here. I'm his mentor. He needed to see me. It was important."

Egypt put her hands on her hips. "Can you tell me what it was about?"

Mr. G adjusted his oval glasses and straightened his tie. "Of course not. You know it's confidential."

"We're here to talk about Egypt," interrupted Mrs. James.

"You're right," said Mr. G as he slid Egypt's grade report to the front of his desk.

Egypt and her mother examined her grades. Egypt hoped that her mother wouldn't notice the zeros, but Mr. G had highlighted them in yellow.

"Why does Egypt have so many missing assignments?" asked Mrs. James, waiting for an explanation.

"Well, Sleepy tends to—" Mr. G began, but Mrs. James

interrupted while Egypt bowed her head and rubbed her amulet, hoping Bastet would save her.

"Excuse me?" said Mrs. James with a look of shock. "Why do you people keep calling my daughter after one of the seven dwarfs? I think you're hurting Egypt's self-esteem."

"I'm sorry," said Mr. G, trying to sound apologetic, "but that's what the other students call her because she sleeps in class."

Mrs. James turned to Egypt. "You have five seconds to explain why you are sleeping in class."

"I'm talking to William on my phone all night," said Egypt in a voice almost as quiet as a mouse. But she didn't want to tell her mother the real reason she was sleepy was that she had been staying up on the internet, trying to find out how to become a dancer for the LD03 so that she could find her father.

"You won't have that problem anymore," snapped Mrs. James as she snatched Egypt's phone out of her hand.

About that time, William appeared in the doorway. Mrs. James, Egypt, and Mr. G turned and looked at him.

"Just the person I need to see," said Mrs. James.

"Mom," said Egypt, trying to stop her mother from showing out.

Mrs. James thought for a second, creating a silence that made everybody uncomfortable. Egypt could hear the gears in her mother's head turning. Then everybody heard a big crash in the back of the room: the skeleton model had crashed to the ground. Sagmus turned around and looked at everybody with the most innocent look on her face.

"Get up here now," said Mrs. James.

Sagmus walked up to the front of the room and sat at a desk. "I'm sorry."

"That's OK," said Mr. G. "I'll fix it when yawl leave."

Then Mrs. James turned her attention back to William. "Would you like to come for Thanksgiving dinner?"

"Yes, ma'am," said William, who ignored Egypt's gesture, indicating he should say no.

"Great, I think I need to get to know the person who is causing my daughter to get such low grades," said Mrs. James.

"Can I help you with something?" interjected Mr. G.

"Do you have that number you told me I could call?" asked William as he approached the desk.

Mr. G opened his middle desk drawer, pulled out a yellow business card, and handed it to William. "Call that number today."

"Excuse me for reaching between you two, ma'am," said William.

"That's fine, but dinner will be at four-thirty next Thursday," said Mrs. James.

"I'll see you then," said William as he hurried away.

Once William left the room, Egypt's parent-teacher conference continued. Mr. G and Mrs. James discussed Egypt's missing assignments in anatomy and physiology, while she stood with her head in her hands, trying to ignore the conversation. However, her head sprang up when she heard that she couldn't participate in the debutante ball dancing practice.

"I'll make up all of my assignments," said Egypt as she still hoped that she could find her daddy for the father-daughter dance of the debutante ball.

"Egypt better or she'll be stuck at home helping her mother clean up the entire house this weekend."

Chapter 16

Egypt woke up from her nap and walked up the stairs to the kitchen. As she entered the dining room, she flipped on the chandelier lights. She pulled the table apart so that she could insert the additional piece to make sure there was enough space for the guests and the food. Egypt went back into the kitchen, and a wave of heat hit her in the face. Mrs. James had opened the oven door to baste the turkey. Egypt reached on the side of the refrigerator and pulled out the extra piece to the dining room table as Mrs. James headed upstairs. After struggling for a few minutes, Egypt finally got the piece in place and set the table with her mother's fine china.

Egypt cut off the lights and walked into the kitchen, where she saw a couple of rolls on a napkin on the table; her mother had made them from scratch. Mrs. James had learned the secret from her mother. She started eating the rolls, but Egypt couldn't even make it into the family room without needing something to drink because the bread made her thirsty. She had to rush back to the kitchen to drink some Russian tea—pineapple juice and tea—before she choked.

As she gulped down the last drop, she noticed a mess in the family room and decided to clean it up. Egypt went to the coffee table, picked up the Scrabble pieces her cousins had left on the floor, and put them into the toy chest next to the TV. She placed the Chinese checkers box on the shelf and straightened out the pillows on the couch. Afterward, she picked up her cup and put it in the sink.

Egypt took the broom from behind the door in the kitchen. She walked down the stairs and swept the crumbs from the floor. When she was done, she put the broom in the corner and sat on the couch. Egypt grabbed a copy of the Thanksgiving newspaper from the coffee table; her mother had bought one from the store earlier. Mrs. James circled the stores she wanted to visit in the morning, the biggest shopping day of the year. Egypt hated to be dragged all over the city shopping the day after Thanksgiving. As soon as she started flipping through the sales advertisements, her mother called her.

"Come here!"

Egypt closed the ads and placed them on the table as she headed upstairs.

"I've got another job for you."

"Mommy," whined Egypt.

"Clean out the fireplace before the guest arrives."

"Where did grandma and grandpa go this time for Thanksgiving?" asked Egypt.

"They went on a cruise down the Nile River," replied Mrs. James.

"I wish they had taken me."

"They took Sagmus with them."

"Darn it! I can't believe that she gets to go to all the cool places."

"Maybe next year, but you need to finish cleaning before William comes, said Mrs. James as she hurried upstairs.

Egypt walked to the fireplace, pulled up the sleeves on her blue sweatshirt, took off her necklace and placed it on top of the mantel, and slid the chain gate open. She picked up the block shovel hanging on the holder along with a small broom and a poker. She placed the shovel back in the fireplace, scooped up a pile of ash, and dumped it into the ash bucket.

Egypt worked as slowly as molasses until her mother gave her some more instructions. "If you don't finish by the time our guests arrive, you're going outside to cut some wood."

Egypt quickened her scoops, dumping all the ash out of the fireplace. She used the small broom to sweep up the ash. Afterward, she picked up some logs from the wood holder. She placed two logs parallel to the bricks in front of the fireplace. Then she put three logs on top, perpendicular to the lower logs. She stuck her head under the fireplace and opened up the flue.

Then she reached up on the mantel and picked up a box of long matches. Egypt scraped the end tip against the side of the box, igniting the match. She lit the ends of the logs in the fireplace.

When she moved away from the flames, she felt her neck was

bare; her amulet was missing. She looked up on the mantel and it wasn't there. "Bastet!"

Egypt's mother came running down the steps in a panic. "What's going on?"

"I lost Bastet," said Egypt as she frantically looked under the box of matches and in between the family pictures on the mantelpiece, almost knocking them down.

"Calm down," said Egypt's mother, trying to keep the situation under control. "I'll help you look for it."

Egypt picked under items on the coffee table, where she had been reading, and on the couch. Her mother glanced around the base of the fireplace, noticed a turquoise semi-stone sticking out in the ash bucket, and pulled it out of the ash. "Here it is," said Mrs. James.

Egypt ran to her mother as fast as she could. "I wouldn't have been able to get through this dinner without it," said Egypt as she squeezed her mother tightly. "My amulet is the gift he left for me on my ninth birthday, when I stood him up for the tea party."

"Do you miss him?"

"Yes, but . . ." Egypt wanted to tell her mother she had seen her father at the Gallery.

"What?" asked Mrs. James

"Nothing," said Egypt.

"I miss him too."

"Why did he leave?"

"It's not easy to explain."

She started, but the doorbell rang, and Mrs. James went

upstairs to answer it. With soot on her face, Egypt walked up the stairs and ran into William. His red leather jacket swirled as she ran past him.

"I'll go check on her," said Mrs. James. "You're welcome to watch the TV in the family room downstairs until dinner is ready."

William walked down the stairs and sat on the couch. He relaxed there for a few minutes before flipping through the magazines on the coffee table. He picked up the remote control and turned on the TV, watching the Turkey Day Bowl. As he sat on the couch, he wondered why he didn't enjoy the sex with Egypt, the most beautiful girl he had ever seen. His father had told him that sleeping with boys was just a phase and a fine woman would cure all that. Yet, all he had been thinking about since that night with Egypt was other guys. After about thirty minutes, Mrs. James called Egypt and William for dinner. William walked upstairs into the dining room and sat down next to Mrs. James.

Out of the corner of his eye, William caught a glimpse of Egypt wearing an embroidered turquoise top, a blue jean skirt, and her bracelet. She came into the room and slid into a chair that faced William.

The turkey sat in the middle of the table on a silver platter with containers of rice, rolls, collard greens, macaroni and cheese, ham, corn bread dressing, cranberry sauce, gravy, broccoli casserole, and corn bread.

"Would you like to say the blessing, William?" asked Mrs. James.

"Sure," said William. "Bless this food we're about to receive, and may it nourish our bodies in Christ's name." Then he shouted, "Amen!"

Egypt scowled at William; she couldn't believe his petulance and ridiculous ending to the blessing.

Mrs. James got out of her seat and cut the turkey with an electric knife, placing slices of the meat on everybody's plates. Egypt served William's fixings from the table.

By the time Egypt and Mrs. James sat down, William had eaten all of his food.

"Yikes," hollered William. "I think that was the best Thanksgiving dinner I've ever had." He wiped his mouth with a silk napkin and gulped down some Russian tea. "Can I have seconds?"

"William," said Egypt, embarrassed that he had asked for more food. "You're acting like you have never eaten before."

"I have to admit I didn't eat today."

"There's plenty," said Mrs. James as Egypt picked over her greens, rice, and turkey. "I'm glad you could join us. I wanted to get to know the young man who has been keeping Egypt on the phone all night."

"Your daughter has been such a good friend to me."

A look of shock came over Egypt's face; she couldn't believe they were still friends after they had sex on the night of the homecoming game.

"Egypt has always been a good listener," said Mrs. James, trying to keep the conversation going. "Would anybody like chocolate cake or sweet potato pie?"

"I'll have both," said William.

Mrs. James handed William a slice of cake and pie on a saucer. "Egypt made the pie," said Mrs. James.

William looked across the table and saw an empty place setting. "Are you all expecting somebody else for dinner?"

"We always set a plate for Egypt's father," said Mrs. James.

"What time is he coming?"

"We don't know. We never know," said Egypt.

"Sounds likes my sperm donor," said William. "I don't remember the last time I saw him." William's phone buzzed. "I need to answer the call," he said as he got up and went into the kitchen.

"Can you believe how he's acting?" whispered Egypt.

"We'll talk about that later," said Mrs. James in a low voice.

William walked back into the dining room. "I need to pick up my mother," he said. "Is it OK if I take her a plate?"

"Sure," said Mrs. James as she filled a Styrofoam plate with food. Egypt and Mrs. James walked William to the door.

"Thanks for inviting me to dinner," he said.

"You're welcome," said Mrs. James.

William walked outside, strapped the plate full of food to the back of his motorcycle, and rode away.

As soon as the door closed, Egypt ran up the stairs to her room.

Chapter 17

Eastside High School had four lunch periods for students to eat their lunch. Egypt ate third lunch outside in the courtyard as she waited for William. She liked how the cold wind felt on her skin. Egypt walked over to the granite table surrounded by benches in the courtyard. Egypt spread a tablecloth on the table and pulled the plates and napkins out of her mother's picnic basket, which included utensils and food.

William took a motorcycle repair class at another school; he spent the morning learning the trade and returned to Eastside during the last lunch. Egypt waited for him, even though she would be thirty minutes late to her class. She wanted to talk to William about being friends, but she hadn't seen or heard from him since Thanksgiving dinner. That hadn't stopped her from bringing extra sandwiches. So Egypt unzipped her lunch bag and began eating a turkey-on-wheat sandwich. As soon as she took a bite, a strong wind blew all the plates, silverware, and cups across the courtyard. Egypt scrambled to pick up all the items. It took her a few minutes to collect them and put them back on the table. She sat back down and felt a cold sensation on her neck. She turned around and saw Paris standing there, smirking.

"What's that?" asked Egypt.

"Huh?" asked Paris, holding a bag behind her back.

"Don't play with me, love."

Paris handed Egypt the bag. Egypt looked inside and grinned. "These are so good!"

"You don't eat junk food."

"I know, but I've been having these weird food cravings lately," said Egypt as she stuffed a handful of fries into her mouth. "Who bought you the food?"

Paris didn't say a word for a moment. "You already know."

"Mr. G takes care of his girl."

Egypt and Paris were so busy eating that they didn't see India and her girls walking toward them. Egypt looked up with a French fry hanging out of her mouth.

"What a cute couple," said India.

Egypt didn't know what to say, but Paris stood up and responded, "We don't swing your way."

"Chubby, I'm going to throw your light-skinned self into a tree," said India in such a harsh voice that Paris lowered herself back onto her seat.

"I don't like that heifer," Egypt whispered to Paris.

"What did you say to me?" asked India as she walked over to Egypt.

"Nothing," said Egypt, her voice cracking.

"I don't mind giving a pretty girl a beatdown," said India.

As India rambled on, Egypt couldn't help but remember when her father had called her pretty on her first daughter's date. She had worn a blue-green dress from Macy's with a green rose that her father gave her as she entered the limo, her carriage. He had worn a blue suit with a green tie to match her outfit. She had loved having her father all to herself that night, but she couldn't believe that her prince had walked out of her life and now she needed him for the father-daughter dance at the debutante ball.

"I'll take it from here," said William as he tapped India on the shoulder.

"No," said India. "I want to do the Christmas Rule."

"You can't," said William. "It has to be me."

India scowled at Egypt. "I can't wait to see your face after school."

"What's she talking about?" asked Egypt as India and her girls walked away.

William sat down next to Egypt. "Paris, would you excuse us?"

"Sure," said Paris as she finished off the fries and walked toward the front of the building.

As soon as Paris was out of sight, Egypt hugged William and started asking him questions. "Where have you been? Why haven't you been at school? Are we just friends?"

"Yikes," said William as he pushed her away.

"I'm sorry," said Egypt. "I just haven't seen you, love."

"I've been busy."

"Too busy to call after we made love?"

"Well, I've slept with many girls."

"Like . . . India?"

"Yeah, but you don't understand."

"Help me understand!"

"India and I used to be an item in the ninth grade, but we broke up around Christmas."

"Why?" asked Egypt.

"Tradition," said William.

"What do you mean?"

"A few years ago, a few members of the LD03 didn't want to buy their girlfriends Christmas presents."

"Ugh," replied Egypt. "I should've known."

"So on the last day before Christmas break, they broke up with their girlfriends."

"You're kidding."

"Nope."

Egypt looked into William's eyes. "Are you a member of the LD03?"

"Not yet."

"What do you mean?"

William reached into his mesh book bag to find something.

"Are you looking for this?" asked Egypt.

"Where did you get that?" asked William as she handed him a green LD03 card that read "You just got dumped."

"This is the one John gave to Paris in the ninth grade," Egypt said.

"I can't believe you're dumping me."

"LD03 made up the Christmas Rule," said Egypt as she walked away and left William staring at the card.

Chapter 18

The sunlight had broken through the blinds, and beams of light fell on Egypt's eyelids, making them twitch. The sounds of Christmas reached Egypt's ears, which made her turn over and pull the covers over her head. Yet, when she heard sausage sizzling and smelled grits boiling and biscuits baking, her eyes popped open. Her stomach growled; she felt like she could eat a horse.

Egypt threw off the covers, lifted her head, and sat up with her feet dangling off the bed. She wanted her grandma's country breakfast, but she kept staring at the pregnancy kit on her desk next to her journal. She had been up all-night writing about William and pondering whether she should take the test. Egypt swung her legs back and forth for a few minutes. Then she slipped on her turtle slippers, walked to her desk, grabbed the kit, and headed to the bathroom to test her urine.

Egypt couldn't believe that Paris had swiped the home pregnancy test from Mr. G's lab, which he had used to demonstrate how nanotechnology can be used as a detector. Paris told her that if he questioned her about it, she would say that she was making sure that she was not expecting. Egypt didn't want to know more. She was glad that Paris had gotten it because her period was late.

Egypt walked into the bathroom door and closed it. She checked the expiration date on the pregnancy test, and it was still valid. She read the instructions several times. Then she washed her hands with warm water and removed the testing device from its foil wrapper. She urinated a little into the toilet before peeing on the stick. Egypt waited five minutes, sitting on the toilet, thinking about why she had given it up so easily. She gathered the strength to look at the result; she picked up the sample stick. A distinct color band was present.

Egypt slipped down and sat on the floor of the bathroom. She couldn't believe that she had gotten pregnant the first time. Then there was a knock on the door.

"Who is it?" asked Egypt.

"Your mother," replied Mrs. James.

Egypt was silent for a few minutes. "Yes, Mother."

"Can you please open the door?"

"I'll be out in a moment."

"OK, I'm wait."

Egypt opened the door with her head hanging down. Her mother walked in and lifted up Egypt's head by placing two fingers under her daughter's chin, revealing her reddish, slightly puffy eyes.

"Do you want to tell me about it?" asked Mrs. James.

"I can't," said Egypt as tears rolled down her face.

"Yes, you can," said Egypt's mother, caressing her daughter's back. "Nothing you do can ever disappoint me."

"I think I'm going to change your mind."

"Tell me and you'll feel better."

"Are you sure?" asked Egypt as she dried her tears.

"Yes," replied her mother.

Egypt sighed. "I'm pregnant."

"OK."

"*That's it?*" asked Egypt, shocked that her mother wasn't more upset.

Mrs. James sat on the bath rug. Egypt joined her on the floor and curled up in her mother's arms. "There's something I never told you," said Mrs. James.

"What?"

"I got pregnant in high school, too."

"By my father?"

"Yes," replied Mrs. James.

"Did you use protection?"

Mrs. James paused for a moment. "We thought I couldn't get pregnant if I was on my period."

"Really?" asked Egypt.

"It doesn't happen that often, but it does occur."

"What should I do about William?"

"Only you can decide that, but I'm here to help."

"I'm scared."

"There's nothing wrong with being afraid."

"I never thought this would happen to me," said Egypt, crying.

"We're going to get through this together."

"I feel so ashamed," said Egypt as she grabbed onto her mother. After a few moments in the bathroom, they walked down the stairs into the living room, where her cousin and her grandmother sat around the Christmas tree.

Wreaths hung on the railing. Mrs. James had hung Christmas cards on the wall along the stairs. A nativity scene was set up on a table at the door that led outside. Sagmus, Egypt's younger cousin, played with a train that sped around the tree a couple of times before it jumped the track. "The Little Drummer Boy" played on the radio. Egypt and her mother reached the bottom of the stairs.

Her grandmother broke the silence. "Merry Christmas."

"Merry Christmas to you, too," said Egypt.

"Let's eat," said Mrs. James. As they headed toward the kitchen, Egypt stopped. "Can we at least open one present now?"

"Sure," said Mrs. James. Egypt, Sagmus, and her grandmother sat on the couch as Mrs. James handed out presents from under the Christmas tree.

Sagmus went first. She got a tan blouse from her grandmother. Egypt's grandmother opened her present; she got tickets to the Alvin Ailey American Dance Theater.

Then Mrs. James opened a small box, and there were keys in it. She went to the window and looked outside; a white Volvo was sitting on the lawn with a red bow on it.

"This is the gift I gave to myself," said Mrs. James.

As Sagmus, Egypt's grandmother, and Mrs. James went outside to look at the Volvo, Egypt carefully unwrapped a small box wrapped in gold paper with a gold bow. After removing the tissue papers, she slid out the jewelry box.

As she opened it, she showed all of her teeth in a huge smile. "Oh!" said Egypt.

"I'm glad you like it," said Egypt's mother, standing in the hallway while Sagmus and her grandmother played with the features of the Volvo.

"Can we eat something?' asked Egypt. "I'm starving."

"Sure," replied Mrs. James. "Since I can't go shopping until tomorrow morning, I might as well enjoy a good meal." The rest of the family came in from outside; they went into the kitchen and had Christmas breakfast.

Chapter 19

The end of winter break brought a mini-ice storm to Stone Mountain. The janitors shoveled the ice from the sidewalk because the principal didn't want any child to get hurt and give parents another excuse to sue the school system. The buses pulled up, and students filed off in their new coats, hats, gloves, and scarves—creating a sanguine mood in the school, at least for a day. Too bad most of the clothes would end up in the lost and found. At the end of the year, the school had so many items that they had a flea market that funded the teachers' end-of-the-school party.

Egypt headed to the band room wanting to talk to Paris about what she should do about the debutante ball now that she was expecting. Her stomach's growls were out of this world. Her doctor told her that she was about two months pregnant and food cravings would go away around the fourth month of her pregnancy. Hopefully, Paris had brought the blueberry-bacon-buttermilk biscuits from Bo's, the culinary arts program's bakery. Her best friend usually went to Mr. G's classroom to help him get ready for the day: writing the objective on the board, placing papers on the desks before the students arrived, and checking each lab station. More than anything, Paris just loved being near Mr. G. Egypt hoped Paris could find a few minutes for her.

Egypt walked into the band room, sat in a seat, and waited for Paris. Students began to walk in, putting their instruments and book bags in their band lockers; they were tired of getting their money stolen from the regular lockers outside. Egypt looked down and picked up a school newspaper with the headline "Chester." A picture of a student kissing a teacher appeared on the front cover; the couple was expressing their love under the Giants of the Mesozoic exhibit at the local natural history museum. The student and teacher didn't notice that their heads were almost dinner for the Tyrannosaurus rex, positioned as they were under its mouth.

But as Egypt took a closer look, she saw that the student had long braids and arched eyebrows. The picture seemed to be . . . Egypt, but the student stood as tall as the teacher. Egypt wished she had that much height; her doctor joked that she could get a handicapped sticker for her car because of her lack of ups. Egypt wondered why somebody had photoshopped her picture onto another girl's body. The complexion of the arms was lighter than Egypt's face and the body looked like a butterball turkey, Paris.

About this time, Paris marched in and walked up to Egypt

with an edition of the *Eastside Eagle* in one hand and a bag of Bo's in the other.

Paris handed Egypt the food and the paper and sat down next to her.

"William," said Paris.

Egypt glanced at the paper again; the tall girl in the picture was chubby. "That's you."

"Yeah . . . how could William do this to us?"

"How do you know it was him?" asked Egypt.

"He works on the newspaper staff."

"Paris, I'm not saying that William didn't do it, but I want to be sure."

Egypt opened the bag and pulled out a biscuit. She took a bite and a swallow of water. She offered Paris a biscuit, but she said no.

"Do you think the sponsor approved the picture on the cover?" asked Egypt.

"No. I talked to the editor. The front page should've been a snap of the girls' basketball team winning the Christmas tournament."

Egypt didn't say a word for a few minutes; she had to squash the growling in her stomach.

She ate another biscuit as Paris rambled on about William. She wiped her mouth with a napkin and asked Paris, "Why did you kiss Mr. G?"

"Well, the Science Club scheduled a trip to the Fernbank IMAX Theatre, but only Mr. G and I showed up. Mr. G didn't want to go to the movie, but I insisted."

"Girl, y'all had a date," said Egypt.

"I just wanted to be treated like a lady . . . for a change."

"What do you mean?"

"Well . . . I've been abused on dates before."

"Boys have hit you?"

"John did."

"I'm so sorry, love," said Egypt. "How many times did it happen?"

"Too many," cried Paris. "But I have a plan for the LD03"

Egypt interrupted. "What is a Chester?"

"A grown man dating a very young girl." Paris laughed.

"Like Mr. G?"

"Nope," said Paris. "Mr. G is in his early twenties, my dating range."

"Tell me about the kiss," said Egypt, trying to change the subject.

A bright smile came over Paris's face. "In a pair of jeans and a sweater, Mr. G didn't look like a teacher. So, after the movie, we walked around the museum holding hands. We stopped in front of the carnivores and kissed; it just happened."

"When did your attraction to Mr. G begin?"

"It started in ninth grade."

"He has been tapping it for that long?"

"No," said Paris giving Egypt a playful hit." "It wasn't until . . ."

"You just told on yourself."

"Anyway. I would just help him before and after school. Stuff like organize his lessons and make sure everything was spelled correctly. After spending so much time with him, I got to know Mr. G more than I realized."

"How?"

"Have you noticed he walks with a slight limp?"

"Not really, but that still doesn't explain why you two hooked up."

"I do things his women never thought about doing."

"Paris, the truth"

"He misses his girlfriend he left in Kenya."

"I didn't know you were so fast."

"At least Mr. G didn't get me pregnant," said Paris as some band members turned around and looked at the girls talking.

"Love, don't try to put the jelly in my plate," said Egypt. "But I wonder why William cropped a picture of me on your body."

"Let's ask him," said Paris, as she noticed William standing in the doorway of the band room.

William unzipped his jacket, pulling down his pants so he showed the top of his underwear. He leaned on the wall and glanced at Egypt. "You like my work?"

Egypt motioned with her finger for William to come to her. He pointed to his chest. Egypt nodded her head.

William made his way toward Egypt, but he tripped and fell flat on his face when his pants fell farther. "Yikes!"

"I can't believe that you are the father of my child," said Egypt as she stood over William, who stopped smiling when he heard the words reach his lips.

Chapter 20

The security guard locked the doors after the final student walked into the building. He could see delivery persons still walking toward the entrance, carrying bouquets of roses, teddy bears, and balloons. When they tried to get into the building, he held up a sign: "No Deliveries Today." Some deliverers became impatient—they were tired of chasing their hats and watching their balloons escape to the heavens. Finally, a slew of police officers showed up and ordered them off school property.

The cafeteria workers brought out packets of ketchup, mustard, and mayonnaise—students would squirt these on the table during lunch—and laid out baskets of hot sauce, salt, and pepper, with salads placed neatly one on top of another. Meanwhile, servers sat at a table sipping coffee, meditating on how to keep the natives—and their sanity—at bay as they worked.

The Men of Eastside, a club pairing boys with men in the community, hung up red and white balloons on the walls, while the detention students rolled in the portable audio system for music during lunch. Meanwhile, the Ladies of Eastside, a club pairing girl with women in the community, roped off a section for the juniors and seniors—their class dues had paid for a specially catered meal. Each student had a place name at their seat. The culinary arts students had cooked baked chicken, fried fish, collard greens, and baked bread and brewed Bewley's black tea.

Egypt and Paris walked into the lunchroom and found the debutantes' table; the girls had rented space to raise money for the debutante scholarship. Egypt carried a tray of white-and-red carnations, tape, and scissors in an old milk crate. The flowers were wrapped in white tissue paper and a red bow. Egypt dropped the crate on the floor next to the table and sat down in a chair.

Paris carried a roll of white paper she had swiped from the library and spread it across the table, while Egypt played on her phone. Paris glared at Egypt, who jumped up when she saw the frown on her face. Egypt held down the paper as Paris wrote out a sign that said "Carnations for Sale." While they were taping the sign to the front of the table and stacking the flowers on top, the bell rang.

LD03 gang members, holding boxes of candy, stood at the entrances of the four hallways leading to the lunchroom, handing out treats to the girls as they entered the cafeteria. Some girls kissed the boys as they gave them the gifts. Other girls refused to take the sweets—they knew that the LD03 expected favors.

Other members of the LD03 sat on the stage eating pizza

alongside the DJ. Paris thought that the LD03 had something on the principal because they were the only group allowed on stage during Valentine's Day. The gifts given out at the door were only the preliminaries—the big event occurred when the LD03 gave out red roses near the end of the period.

The freshmen girls crowded the stage as if at a concert—pushing, kicking, and stepping on one another for the ideal rose-jockeying position. These roses, of course, gave them entry to the LD03 fashion show, where Chesters, grown men who slept with young girls, would give them jewelry, clothes, and money.

"Girl, how are we going to get business if the LD03 are giving out candy?" asked Egypt.

"Actually, we'll get more business from t.he girls' boyfriends," replied Paris.

"Love, I'm a little slow. Can you explain that?"

"They'll buy a flower from us because they don't want their girlfriends getting anything from the LD03."

A roar came from one entrance, and a sea of balloons floated toward the debutantes' table. Every girl thought it was their boyfriend bringing the items—hoping they had read their minds and knew exactly what they wanted for Valentine's Day. Maybe the stories in romance novels were true!

The balloons covered the person's face, but Egypt could see that he wore red jeans. When the balloons got to the table, William stepped forward and said, "I'm sorry."

"That's cute," said Paris.

Egypt walked to William and used her pinkie to push back his head. "I'm still mad at you for what you did to Paris and me."

"I know," said William.

"How could you treat the mother of your child that way?"

"Guys do stupid things. That's what we do."

Many of the young ladies around the table shook their heads in agreement. "That's a sorry excuse," said Egypt.

"How can I make it up to you?" asked William.

Before he could answer, members of the LD03 pushed their way through the crowd and surrounded Egypt and William. The gang members formed a singing group with William as the lead singer. The DJ handed William the microphone; he got down on one knee and sang a love song to Egypt.

About that time, the LD03 members moved to the stage, where John announced that they were about to give out roses. The ninth-grade girls ran to the stage in a frenzy, begging for the blooms.

Egypt folded her arms. "Love, I know what you can do."

"What?" replied William.

"Get me an LD03 rose!"

"Yikes!" said William as the young ladies at the stage shouted. "Only John gives out roses."

"That's what I want."

William headed toward the stage as the chants for the roses became louder. John walked to the back of the stage and picked up some roses from a bucket. He moved to the front of the stage and turned his back to the crowd, where the screaming was at a fevered pitch. He took the roses and tossed them over his head. The girls scrambled for them, tearing weaves from one another's hair. John turned and saw William sneaking a rose out of the bucket and gave William a wink.

Girls in the crowd continued to fight over the roses, while William walked back—with a rose—toward the debutantes' table.

Paris looked at Egypt in amazement. "Do you know what that means?"

"Yes," said Egypt. "But I wanted one because my father used to give them out on Valentine's Day." When William gave Egypt the rose, she gave him her best kiss ever.

India's voice boomed over the cafeteria; she stood on the stage with the DJ's microphone in her hand. "Egypt has a rose!"

"Time to go!" said Paris as she grabbed Egypt, and they flew out the lunchroom doors. A stampede of girls ran after them.

Chapter 21

Eastside High School hadn't won a state championship in years; tonight, however, the girls' basketball team had a chance to win their first state trophy in the school's history. They would face their archrival, Westside High, which was the reigning champion five years running. Egypt attended the game to sneak into the LD03 fashion show, which took place in a private box at the arena. She wore her LD03 rose on her blouse.

The previous game had just ended, and the scouts from the SEC, ACC, and the Big Ten took a bathroom break before the game between the Eastside Eagles and the Westside Vikings. The trainers moved the rack of basketballs onto the court so the teams could warm up, while the arena workers swept the floor with large brooms—like at a WNBA game. The cheerleaders from both teams placed their pom-poms and megaphones at the opposite ends of the court. The mascots—in full costume—met at half-court, jeering at each other.

The fans filled in the seats behind their teams. Egypt and Paris walked down the steps of the Eastside section and sat a few rows behind the student cheer group, the Traveling Pep Rally. They had jeered the Vikings' cheerleaders so badly during a home game at Eastside that the high school administrators banned the group from entering when the Hawks visited the Vikings in the final game of the season.

The Eastside players appeared in the tunnel of the arena wearing their purple warm-ups, shoes, and socks. The point guard dribbled onto the court, followed by the rest of the girls. She led the team to half-court, sped toward the basket, and shot the basketball off the side of the fiberglass. The other players repeatedly pushed the ball against the backboard until they got to the last player of the team, who made the basket. The Eastside coaches marched in with their clipboards and sat down on their bench near the scorer's table.

Another roar came from the crowd; the Westside Vikings had come onto the court. The players wore white shorts, jerseys, socks, and tennis shoes. The team conducted defensive drills, with two players at a time simulating one-on-one plays, while the coaches ran up and down the sideline, hollering at the players to be more aggressive. After completing the drills, the Vikings lined up around the foul line and took shots.

The officials called the captains to the center of the court. While the referees talked to the captains, the players from both teams huddled on the benches. After the meeting, the lights in the arena were dimmed, and an array of lights rotated around the building as music reverberated everywhere. The benchwarmers formed two rows for the starters to run through. As each name was called, the players ran past their teammates and shook the hands of the opposing coaches.

The crowd stood up when the ROTC unit marched to the center of the floor and displayed their colors. As the crowd sang "The Star-Spangled Banner," the players put their hands over their hearts. After the anthem, the crowd cheered with excitement. The two teams huddled, making a circle that swayed from one side to another, pumping each other up. At the tip-off, Eastside's center tipped the ball to #23, who dunked the basketball but fell on her ankle.

The trainers, along with the coaches, rushed to attend to Eastside's star player. For several minutes the forward lay face down on the floor, unmoving. The trainers whispered into her ear and rubbed her back. Slowly, the injured player started to move her legs and arms. She turned over and sat up. The Eastside fans went wild.

The injured player hopped to the bench, refusing to let the coaches help her. Along the way she pumped her fist in the air, keeping the crowd fired up. When she got to the bench, she sat in a chair. The trainers took off a sock and shoe, sprayed her ankle with an aerosol, and propped it up on a bag of ice.

Egypt looked over at Paris. "Love, is she going to play?"

"Yeah," replied Paris.

"How can you be so sure?" said Egypt with a look of confusion. "She gets hurt every game."

Egypt and Paris watched the Vikings score several baskets in a row. "Girl, she better get well soon before we get too far behind."

Suddenly, the crowd screamed and stood up; Eastside's star

player had reported to the scorer's table. The Vikings knocked the ball out of bounds, and the referee let #23 back into the game.

As soon as the ball was put into play, her teammates passed the ball to #23, who hit a three-pointer. The Traveling Prep Rally woke up, jeering the other team so loud that Egypt and Paris could barely hear themselves. With their star player in the game, Eastside started catching up—by halftime, the game was tied. Egypt and Paris walked to the concession stand and bought some French fries. As they ate their food, a cheerleader from Westside came up to Paris and hugged her.

"You disappeared on me," said Paris. "What happened?"

Lisa replied, "William."

"Excuse me?" said Egypt.

"Who's this?" asked Lisa.

"She's my best friend," said Paris. "And she's kind of dating William."

"I used to be your BFF," said Lisa.

"Yeah, until you fell off the planet last summer," said Paris, still wondering why Lisa hadn't called her.

"I know y'all want to catch up on old times," said Egypt, "but can we get back to William?"

"Did you sleep with him?" asked Lisa.

"Maybe." Egypt stared at Lisa for a moment and then looked away. "How can you tell?"

"You look about two months pregnant."

"Something like that."

"Then William passed his last test for membership into the

LD03 by deflowering a girl," said Lisa. "And he may be HIV positive."

"Oh my God. William has AIDS?" shouted Egypt as curious faces turned their way. "How can you be sure?"

"Last spring the health department contacted me; the blood I donated at the school tested positive for the virus," said Lisa.

"Did you tell William?" asked Egypt.

"I tried, but his phone number was disconnected."

"Have you seen William today?" asked Egypt.

"Yeah," replied Lisa. "He's working at the LD03 fashion show."

"Where?" asked Egypt.

Lisa showed Egypt and Paris the direction. "Thank you," Egypt said as she dragged Paris toward him. The girls approached William, who was sitting at a table in front of a private luxury box.

"Yikes!" said William. "What are you doing here?"

"Looking for you," said Egypt.

Suddenly, a rush of bodyguards came through the breezeway with a man in the middle. Egypt stared at him and tried to break through the men, but William held her back. She screamed, "Daddy!"

The man stopped and said, "Egypt!" Before he could reach for her, his bodyguards forced him out of the arena.

"Why did you stop me?" cried Egypt.

"He's the LD03 leader!" said William.

Chapter 22

Egypt felt a tumbling motion in her stomach that woke her up. She could feel the baby moving around. Then she heard a ding on her phone. She picked it up and saw a text from William; she had forgotten that he had added her to the LD03 text group. The text was an invitation to the spring break pool party at International Park. The venue had been built for the 1996 Atlanta Olympic Summer Games beach volleyball competition. After the Olympics, the facility was turned into a water park, and the Lakeview Complex used it for music events. William had taken Egypt to several Thursday-night concerts, where they sat out on the lawn, listened to music, and sipped on sparkling grape juice.

Egypt decided to check out the pool party, so she jumped out of bed and put on some clothes. Their house was so big that her mother never heard anything coming from Egypt's room. Egypt walked downstairs, took the keys off the hook, and went into the garage.

Egypt pulled the emergency cord on the garage door and pulled it open. She got into the car, released the emergency break, and put the car in neutral. Then she stepped out of the Bug and gave it a slight push backward. Luckily, she jumped into the car and closed the door just before it hit the garage doorframe. The car rolled down the hill, and Egypt turned the steering wheel so that the car turned into the street. She started the car and headed out of the subdivision.

As Egypt approached the entrance to the park, cars were backed up on the highway, trying to get into the party that LD03 held every night. The cars inched along at a snail's pace. So Egypt read one of the debutante magazines her mother had given her, but she didn't see how she would ever get to the debutante ball now that she was pregnant. She became so engrossed in the stories of debutantes that she didn't notice a policeman walk up to her car. The officer tapped on the window with his flashlight, and she rolled down the window.

"What's going on?" asked Egypt.

"Can I see your invitation?"

Egypt grabbed her phone and gave it to the officer, displaying the invite. He snatched the device and looked at it. "You must be excited."

"Why?"

"Because you're twelve hours early; the pool party doesn't start until five p.m."

"Oh, gosh darn it!"

"Come back in the afternoon and you'll have plenty of customers."

"OK."

Egypt moved out of line and headed home, driving along with ease in the opposite direction, but she still could see cars backed up on the other side of the highway, trying to get to the LD03 party. Her car ran so quietly that she was able to drive into the garage without her mother hearing her. Egypt turned off the car, closed the garage door, and sneaked upstairs to her room. Before falling asleep, she sent a text to Paris: *Meet me at my house at noon.*

In the morning Egypt's mother opened Egypt's bedroom door, grabbed the trash can, and went downstairs. Mrs. James came back into the room and put the empty can next to Egypt's desk. She walked into the hallway and dragged the vacuum cleaner into the room. She started vacuuming, hitting the hose against the bed, sucking up paper clips, and picking up pieces of hole-punched paper that Egypt had left on the floor after organizing her notebooks. Egypt tried to drown out the noise by putting her hands over her ears, but she finally gave up and removed the covers from her head.

Egypt hollered, "Mom!"

Mrs. James cut off the vacuum and smiled at Egypt, who was sitting up in bed. "Did you say something?"

"Can I go to the beach today?"

"Sure," said Mrs. James, "if you finish your chores."

"I don't have time," said Egypt as she peeked at her watch,

•

not believing she had been asleep for so long. "Paris will be here any moment."

"How can y'all leave in a few minutes when you haven't even gotten out of bed?"

Egypt jumped up and ran to her closet. She pulled out a pair of jeans and put them on. Next, she reached into her drawer, pulled out a shirt, and stretched it over her head. The doorbell rang.

"Paris," said Egypt as she ran downstairs.

"Maybe she can help you with your chores," said Mrs. James, knowing that her daughter didn't hear her.

Egypt opened the door and dragged Paris into the kitchen. "You have to help me."

"With what?" asked Paris.

Before Egypt could answer, Mrs. James interrupted. "Egypt tells me that y'all are going to the beach?"

"That's correct," said Paris.

"Egypt has work to do before she can go."

"Mrs. James, I thought you liked me," said Paris.

"I do," said Egypt's mother. "That's why you're going to help clean my house."

"Why can't Sagmus wash the dishes?" asked Egypt.

"You paid her to do them last time."

"I forgot about that."

"I'll wash the dishes," said Paris.

"Then I'll clean the toilets," said Egypt.

Egypt walked up the stairs to the bathroom. She flipped on the light. The trash overflowed with tissue paper, Q-tips, and dental floss. She pulled the bag out of the trash can and sat it outside the door. She reached under the sink, got another bag, and put it into the can. Then Egypt sprayed the toilet with a cleaner and wiped it down, including the bottom edges on the floor. Finally, she scrubbed the sink and cleaned the mirror.

Egypt ran downstairs and cleaned the first-level bathroom. She went into the kitchen and saw Paris sitting in a chair listening to music with her earphones in her ears. "What are you doing?"

"Letting the dishes soak," replied Paris.

"Love, why do you think we have a dishwasher?"

Egypt opened the door of the appliance and pulled out the top tray. She put the cups on the top row as Paris handed them to her. After finishing the cups, Egypt pushed that tray into the dishwasher and pulled out the bottom tray. The girls rinsed off the plates and placed them in the machine. Egypt pushed the bottom tray into the dishwasher and put a triple-action soap into the dispenser cup. She slammed the door shut and flipped on the switch while making sure that the hot prewash had been selected.

The girls sat down and took a break. "I'm tired," said Egypt.

Mrs. James walked into the room. "I checked your work and it will pass on a sliding scale."

"So we can go?" asked Egypt.

"Yes," replied Mrs. James.

Egypt and Paris got their stuff and jumped into Paris's car. As they put on their seat belts and headed down the driveway, Paris asked Egypt, "Why are we leaving so freaking early? The show doesn't start for another three hours!"

"I need to find out the truth about William."

Egypt grabbed a white bag next to her. She reached in and pulled out a hamburger.

"What are you doing?" asked Paris.

"I'm starving," replied Egypt.

"You don't eat red meat!"

"I'm so hungry I could eat a horse," said Egypt. "Plus, I'm eating for two."

"On the way home, you're buying me some more food."

"No problem, and maybe we could get some more of these burgers," said Egypt as they sat in traffic. Finally, the girls approached the gates of International Park, and the officer waved Paris into the lot after she showed him her LD03 invitation.

"How did you get an invitation?" asked Egypt.

"John; he's never taken me off the LD03 group text," replied Paris.

After parking, Egypt and Paris walked the outside perimeter of the complex along the fence until they found a place where they could see inside. A big slide swirled down into the water. Along the beach was a long row of lounge chairs and picnic tables full of food. In the water, members of LD03 tried to play volleyball, but each time a ball crossed the net, they kept dunking one another. The lifeguard tried to get them to stop, but they ignored him.

William had been lying on a lounge chair but walked over to the table and picked up a hamburger. John came up behind him and tapped William on the butt. William turned around and gave John a kiss on the lips.

"Oh my!" said Egypt.

"Were you expecting that?" asked Paris.

"Not really, but I've seen enough. I think it's time to go."

"You're right, love."

Egypt turned around right into the arms of a man; she looked up and screamed "Daddy!" She hugged him as tight as she could for several minutes. Finally, she softened her grip long enough for Mr. James to see a stream of tears rolling down her face. He handed her his business card and put his finger up to his mouth to signal that she shouldn't make a sound.

"Egypt, it's not safe for you here," said Mr. James.

"I don't understand," said Egypt.

"This is not the time," said Mr. James. "But I'll explain everything soon."

"When?"

"I always know where you are and who you're with," said Mr. James. "Paris, please take Egypt home."

"Sure," said Paris as a security guard approached them.

Egypt and Paris walked toward the car as Mr. James stepped in front of the guard. "Where are those two going?" asked the guard.

"I sent them home."

"Why?"

"They're sixteen, too old."

Chapter 23

Egypt's family drove to the Easter Monday celebration at the Kirkwood United Methodist Church. Passersby often missed the edifice because the church sign was so faded that it couldn't be read from the street. The building had four pillars representing the four pillars of faith: social justice, community, spirituality, and simplicity. The three steps at the front of the church connected these pillars to the body of Christ, all the churches around the world.

Egypt's family finally reached the church. They had to wait until all of the floats had passed in the Easter Monday Parade. As soon as Egypt's mother's car stopped, Sagmus jumped out of the car. She ran up the stairs and joined her Sunday school crew, a group of fourth graders playing tag. Mrs. James had tried to catch her to keep her from dirtying her clothes as Sagmus circled around the Lenten Roses planted near the pillars of the church. But finding herself out of breath, Mrs. James had decided to start gossiping with the members of her choir instead of chasing her niece.

As Egypt sat in her mother's SUV, she replayed the kiss between William and John in her mind. She couldn't believe she was impregnated by a boy who liked other boys. After sitting in the vehicle for a while, thinking about her the baby growing in her stomach, she reluctantly got out of the car and strode across the parking. Egypt walked up to the entrance of the church. Egypt went inside and sat in a pew, wondering how she could've fallen in love with William.

Her mother came in and sat down next to her. "What's the matter, dear?"

Egypt lay her head in her mother's lap. "I found out the truth about William," she said as tears filled her eyes.

"Isn't that what you wanted?" asked Mrs. James.

"Yeah, but he's still the father of my child."

"The truth is hard to handle."

"That sounds like a sermon," said Egypt. "Are you preaching next Sunday?"

"I'll think about it," Mrs. James said with a smile. "Do you want to join the Easter egg hunt outside?"

"Yes, but I want to pray first."

"I'll leave you alone."

Mrs. James walked out of the sanctuary, and Egypt slowly made her way to the altar. The cloth from Sunday's communion still covered part of the altar, where the communion cups were inserted. Egypt looked up at the picture of Jesus that was hanging over the choir stand before falling on her knees and praying. She prayed as hard as she could. "Please God protect my baby and make him strong and healthy. Also, please help my father show up for the father-daughter dance of the debutante ball."

Egypt felt a person kneel next to her. She opened her eyes and couldn't believe who was at the altar. "What are you doing here?" she squealed.

People in the sanctuary turned around and looked at the couple. "Could you lower your voice?" asked William.

"Sure, but shouldn't you be with your boyfriend?"

"What's that supposed to mean?"

"I think you understand."

". . . Can we go somewhere and talk?"

Egypt grabbed William by the hand and dragged him through the doors of the sanctuary to the youth classroom. Egypt and William sat down on the carpet.

Egypt looked at William for a few minutes but looked away when it felt like he was looking into her soul.

"You are so pretty," said William, ". . . especially when you're mad."

"Don't play," said Egypt.

"I can't change what I am."

"I could care less if you like boys," said Egypt. "I'm lying . . . I care, but . . . why didn't you tell me?"

"You don't understand," said William.

"I deserve the truth!"

"It's not that simple."

"To me it is," said Egypt with her hand on her hip. "Are you gay or not?"

William looked at Egypt, and this time she didn't look away as he gazed into her dark eyes. "I'm not sure."

"What do you mean?"

"I care about you, but boys get me excited."

"And me?"

Before William could answer, a drone flew into the room, almost hitting him. He jumped up from his seated position and swatted at the drone. The flying object chased him back into the sanctuary. He ran in and out of pews until he ran out of the back of the church, almost hitting the pastor, with the drone hot on his tail. Egypt looked up in the balcony and saw Sagmus with one of her friends, holding a remote control and laughing. Egypt stared at Sagmus until she stopped smiling and handed the control over to her buddy. She walked down from the balcony to Egypt.

"Love, why did you do that?" Egypt asked Sagmus when she sat next to her on a pew in the front of the church.

"Because he's treated you so bad," replied Sagmus.

"Love, thank you, but I have to tell your parents."

"They don't care—they're too busy traveling the world."

Egypt and Sagmus joined the Easter egg hunt. Some eggs were in bushes; others had been placed in the grass, trees, and windowpanes. Egypt helped Sagmus collect more than a dozen. Afterward, they sat on the church steps and opened the plastic containers; dollar bills fell out. Egypt had forgotten that the preacher gave out blessings.

CHAPTER 24

As the students headed to class, they were in a frenzy over the "Chester Pool." They were betting big bucks on whether the teacher who had been caught kissing a student would get fired or go to jail—or both. A picture of the incident had been published in the newspaper, which inspired the LD03 to organize the jackpot that had quickly reached several thousand dollars.

Egypt rushed into the main office huffing and puffing. The baby was applying pressure on her lungs, making her work harder to breathe. She bumped into the counter, almost knocking over the girls' basketball team's state championship trophy. She took a seat outside the principal's office, opened her book bag, pulled out her inhaler, and took a few puffs. That settled her down. She sat quietly as the secretary took phone calls, wrote out late notes, typed a letter for the principal, greeted parents, fussed at kids, and received the leftovers from the morning concessions—biscuits, orange juice, honey buns, and hot chips. Mr. G came in and sat in the chair next to Egypt, with sweat rolling down his face.

The door to the principal's office opened, making Egypt jump a little in her seat. He motioned for Egypt and Mr. G to come inside. When they entered, they saw an administrator seated at the principal's desk, and Egypt's mother was standing next to him under a picture of the school's faculty.

The musty smell of the principal's office made Egypt's chest tighten, and the room started to close in on her. She took out her inhaler again and took a few more puffs. It provided some comfort but only for a few minutes. Then the adults started talking.

As the administrator talked, Egypt thought he was trying to sound like one of the judges on TV, reading some official-sounding words as if they were in a courtroom. Egypt listened to the charges against Mr. G and realized he had been accused of having a relationship with a student in the past. The administrators wanted him to confess to the inappropriate relationships. Egypt didn't know about the other charges, but she knew from what Paris had told her that they were a couple.

"Who are we waiting for?" asked Egypt as she stared at the empty chair in the room.

Before the adults could answer, the door opened, and William entered. He was wearing a red hat, jeans, and a white shirt. "Sorry I'm late," he said as he took his seat in the empty chair.

Egypt glanced at William, but he stared straight ahead, not

paying attention to his baby's mamma. When the administrator, sitting at the principal's desk, glared at William, he removed his cap.

"Thank you," said the administrator as he took a few minutes to write some notes in his folder. "This is an official hearing to determine if Mr. G had a sexual relationship with Egypt James."

"I can't believe that a teacher would sleep with a student," interrupted William. "He's probably the one that's been recruiting girls to dance at the Gallery," he said, and then he winked at the administrator.

"How could you say that after all he's done for you?" asked Egypt.

"Mr. G shouldn't be doing stuff like that," said William.

Egypt and William continued to make verbal jabs at each other as Mrs. James and

Mr. G stood between the couple.

"Hold on," said the administrator as he stood up in front of the principal's desk. "If both of you don't settle down, y'all will be going to alternative school."

The administrator continued the hearing and explained the format. "Everybody in the room will testify. If I find enough evidence to support the charge, I'll refer the matter to the Internal Affairs Department."

Egypt tried to follow what the people in the room were saying, but she struggled to breathe. Mr. G sweated profusely as he explained his side of the story in a cracked monotone the others could barely hear. William told the principal that somebody sent him the picture via email, and he just imported it into the newspaper article. He didn't notice that Mr. G and a student were kissing in the photograph. Afterward, the adults engaged in intellectual feints while Egypt's airways tightened.

All of sudden, Paris burst into the proceedings. "Don't convict my man!" she screamed as Egypt fell to the floor from lack of air to her lungs.

"My baby!" hollered Mrs. James as she rushed to comfort her child. Then she turned to the administrator and said, "Call 911!"

The administrator picked up the phone and dialed for help. Then he ordered Paris, Mr. G, and William out of the room. Mrs. James calmed her daughter down; she told her to take two puffs on her inhaler every two minutes for about ten minutes. Her breathing got faster at first, but eventually, Egypt began to breathe normally again. The administrator went over to his cooler next to his mini-refrigerator, dispensed some water into a cup, and gave it to Egypt. She took a few sips.

"Thank you," said Egypt. "The baby is kicking up a storm."

"I'm glad to hear that," said Mrs. James.

The paramedics arrived and lifted Egypt onto the gurney. "Be careful; she's pregnant," said Egypt's mother. The paramedics placed a mask over Egypt's mouth and let her breathe some oxygen. Afterward, they gently put the straps over Egypt, adjusted the height of the gurney, and rolled it out of the room. Mrs. James followed the paramedics as they moved Egypt out of the school.

Chapter 25

The naked dogs ran in her head; Egypt couldn't believe they had returned. She hadn't seen them in so long that she had thought about posting a "Lost Dog" sign in her neighborhood and offering a reward. They even had strings—something her dogs always came with when her father brought them to her. Egypt's eyes began to flutter. Her soul fought to keep her asleep, but the light pulled her into the world. As she rolled over in her bed, she could see the fuzzy outline of the naked dogs and strings on the tray next to her bed—two hot dogs with ketchup and a pile of French fries, along with a Varsity Orange milkshake.

The nurse then pulled the covers back over Egypt's body and raised the thermostat to make sure it wasn't too cold, checked the arterial line, read the heart monitor, tested the intravenous restraints, and watched the ventilator rise and fall.

The nurse left the room quietly, but the sound of the door closing jolted Egypt's eyes open; she realized she was not dreaming. There were naked dogs in the room; she could smell them. Then a frightening thought popped into her head as she stared at her stomach and asked, "Where's my baby?"

Egypt sat up in her bed, scanned the room, and removed the IVs from her arms. Alarms started blaring, but Egypt ignored them, frantically searching the room for her baby. She looked under the bed, in the closet and bathroom, around the rocking chair, behind the curtains, and in the cabinets.

Mrs. James had been sleeping in a chair, but the noise woke her. She jumped up, grabbed Egypt, and asked, "What's wrong?"

"Where's my baby?" asked Egypt, panicked.

"Calm down . . . He's fine."

"Is everything OK?" the head nurse asked as she burst into the room.

"Yes," answered Mrs. James as the nurse reattached all the equipment. Mrs. James sat Egypt on the bed and explained, "The doctors decided to take the baby."

"Why?" asked Egypt.

"They thought it would be best after they examined you," said Mrs. James.

"Can I see my baby?"

"Sure."

"Who brought me the naked dogs?" asked Egypt.

"I think you know!"

"Why didn't he stay long enough for me to ask him about the debutante ball?" asked Egypt, her eyes watering.

"I don't know," Egypt's mother sighed. "Do you want to see Baby James?"

"Sure."

Mrs. James helped Egypt into a wheelchair and rolled her down the hall past the nurse's desk. As she approached the observation window, she saw William looking at the babies in the neonatal intensive care unit. She nearly leaped out of her chair, but Mrs. James held her down and rolled her a few feet away from him. She talked to Egypt for a few minutes, which seemed to settle her down.

When Mrs. James pushed Egypt near William, she whispered in her ear, "Remember what we talked about."

"Yes, Mother," said Egypt. She looked up at William and asked, "What are you doing here?"

William continued to stare into the window. The nurse smiled at the baby while placing one hand on his head and the other at his feet. A blanket with red, white, and blue stripes covered Baby James. He rolled onto his side, but it didn't disturb the feeding tube in his mouth or the IV in his arm. The couple could see a red wave traveling across the screen of the heart monitor. Finally, William turned back to Egypt and said, "I'm here to see my son."

"You were never interested in the baby before," Egypt scoffed.

"Things change," said William. "What's his name?"

"Baby James."

"Why do you call him that?"

"I haven't had a chance to give him a name."

"Why?"

"The doctor delivered the baby by cesarean."

"What's that?"

"That's when the doctors stick a huge needle in your back and make incisions to deliver the child."

William shivered "Did it hurt?"

"I don't remember. They put me to sleep."

The nurse and Mrs. James walked up to Egypt as William continued to watch his son squirm in the crib.

"The doctor needs to talk to you," said Mrs. James.

"Can it wait?"

"I'm afraid not."

"Will you be here when I get back?" Egypt asked William.

"Nothing can pry me away from this window."

The nurse wheeled Egypt back to her room. Mrs. James held the door to Egypt's room open as the nurse pushed her inside. The nurse helped Egypt onto the bed by picking up both of her legs. Egypt's mother sat down in the chair in front of the bed.

The nurse fluffed the pillow as Egypt leaned forward, then gently pushed her back so she could rest. The nurse turned on the television, and Egypt flipped to her favorite soap opera. Egypt's mother turned a couple of pages of a magazine, pretending to read.

The nurse started to leave the room but stopped halfway through the doorway. "The doctor will be coming to talk to you in a few minutes."

"About what?" asked Egypt.

"She'll tell you more," said the nurse.

"Mommy . . ." cried Egypt as Mrs. James got up and hugged her daughter.

The doctor walked into the room carrying a clipboard. "I'm Dr. Harris and I delivered your baby."

"Why did you take him so early?" asked Egypt.

"Delivering him by C-section gave him the best chance of survival."

"Will he be OK?"

"With a preemie, there are always risks," said the doctor. "I want to make sure you're aware of that."

"Thank you for telling me the truth."

"Something else has come up," said the doctor.

"What?" asked Egypt.

"I saw you talking to William."

"And . . ."

"He often brings patients to our hospital."

"What types of patients?" asked Egypt.

"Young girls . . . in your condition."

"He has more children?"

"I don't know if he's the father of the other girls' babies," said the doctor, "but he usually pays the bill with an LD03 credit card."

"How do you know about the LD03?"

"It paid for this neonatal intensive care unit."

Chapter 26

The Grim Reaper, dressed in a cloak and carrying a scythe, leaned over two bodies lying on the hood of a smashed-up car as the students marched into the auditorium. The teachers had forced all the juniors into "Ghost Out," a program about drinking and driving. Mr. G's substitute threatened the smart students, who wanted to go to the library, by suggesting they would be written up if they didn't attend. The car had been crashed by a drunk driver, but when the eleventh graders saw their friends, they ignored the activities on the stage and began socializing.

The administrator tried to get the attention of the students, but they joked and laughed. Finally, they settled down, sat down, and quieted down. A representative from Ghost Out explained the program and talked to the students about the dangers of consuming alcohol before getting behind the wheel of a car. To emphasize their point, a female teacher brought out an Eastside student onto the stage; he had been in an alcohol-related accident after a school dance and was now in a wheelchair.

The crowd gasped. The student had been one of the stars of the basketball team and a favorite among the young ladies at the school. As the program continued, the students chattered among themselves about their fallen hero. Egypt, who had been standing in the back of the auditorium, took this time to slip out. She walked down the hall and into Mr. G's room. She grabbed the keys off the hook near the projector screen and started to leave just as she heard a creaking sound. Egypt took off running.

Soon she stopped in the hallway, wondering what had happened. After thinking about it for a few minutes, she peeked around the corner into the classroom. The gray overhead screen had fallen to the floor. Apparently, the paper clips holding the screen had given way. Egypt decided to put the screen back up, so she dragged a chair from a table and pushed it up near the blackboard. She hooked up one side of the screen and then the other. She felt kind of proud: It looked better than before it had fallen.

However, a touch of sadness took away her joy when a book about caring for babies lying on the table caught her attention, a text used in the Eastside childcare program. Egypt started thinking about her baby in intensive care and started crying; her child needed her mother. How in the world could she take care of another human being?

Egypt picked up the book and headed for the computer lab, where Paris sat outside the door, eating a Big Mac, fries, a chocolate shake, and an apple pie. "That's a lot of food," said Egypt.

"A girl has to eat," said Paris as she took a bite of her hamburger and stuffed some fries into her mouth. "What took you so long?"

"You don't want to know," said Egypt.

"Do you have the key?"

Egypt dropped the book on the floor. She turned the pockets of her jeans inside out. "I thought I put it in my pocket."

"You lost it?"

"Darn it . . . it must've fallen out when I fixed the projector."

"I have a backup plan," said Paris. She pulled a screwdriver out of her purse.

"Love, why do you have that?"

Paris stared at Egypt for a minute, not wanting to tell her the truth, but she came clean: "There've been times I've needed to get into the lab and couldn't find Mr. G."

Paris took the screwdriver and placed it near the faceplate of the door. She pushed on the latch bolt. As Paris worked, the girls heard the footsteps of the principal; his shoes always made a clicking sound on the floor.

"Hurry up!" said Egypt.

The lock popped. The girls grabbed their stuff and rushed inside. They heard the principal walk up to the door and turn the doorknob, but a call on the radio stopped him from walking into the room. The girls could hear the principal walk away.

Egypt and Paris sat on the floor of the computer room for a few minutes with their ears to the door. After they were sure that the principal had left, the girls leaned their backs against the wall and rested for a moment. Egypt flipped through the pages of her book while Paris finished eating her food.

"Love, why do you eat so much junk food?" asked Egypt.

Paris sighed. "I've been stressing over grades since I was in ninth grade and food is how I dealt with the pressure. My parents only want As, all other grades are Fs to them."

"I think my mother didn't push me that much because my father had left us."

"After having sex with John, I went crazy," said Paris.

"What do you mean?" asked Egypt.

"I lost interest in everything... I was like a zombie on those TV shows that have been on forever; I wandered aimlessly my entire tenth grade year. Also, I felt dirty, and I tried to drown myself in food to forget what happened in ninth grade. Yet, I like dating older men because they treat me like a lady."

"OK," said Egypt. "I can't believe you can pick a lock," said Egypt.

"You don't want to know what else I can do," said Paris. "I even taught Mr. G how to . . ."

"Paris," said Egypt in a condescending tone. "Both of you should be ashamed of yourselves."

"I know, but let's focus on the immediate problem: We need escorts for the debutante ball."

"Tell me how this works, love."

Paris got up from the floor and turned on a computer. She walked over to the bulletin board while the computer booted up. Egypt joined her, and Paris pointed to the teenescort.com flyer offering escorts to debutante balls. Egypt and Paris went back to the computer. They sat down in the chairs next to the computer as it finished booting up.

The icons on the desktop came up on the screen. Paris clicked on a browser and typed in "www.teenescort.com." Then she entered her username and password for her account, and her dashboard appeared.

"YOU ALREADY HAVE A DATE!" screamed Egypt.

Paris turned to Egypt. "I think they heard you on the top of Stone Mountain—can you keep it down?"

"OK," said Egypt. "How many guys did you talk to?"

"One," said Paris.

"Why?"

"The first guy's profile sounded so cute." Paris blushed.

"Are you that easy?"

"LOOK! Mr. G's arrest freaked me out, and I submitted my credit card information before I came to my senses."

"You have a credit card?" asked Egypt.

"My father may not be a big shot lawyer like your mother, but he takes care of his girls."

"I would trade in my mother's law degree to have a father like yours."

Paris and Egypt surfed the website for escorts and clicked on several profiles. Many of the clips had the girls laughing on the floor at the boys who thought they were doing the young ladies a favor by being their escorts. Finally, Egypt and Paris clicked on a profile that caught their attention, and they smiled at each other.

Paris handed Egypt her credit card and broke the silence. "He's fine."

"Ain't that the truth," said Paris.

Egypt requested an escort. She filled in her personality information, typed in Paris's credit card number, and pressed the "submit" button.

"Check your email when you get home," said Paris.

"I can't believe I got an escort for the ball on the internet."

"It's amazing!"

"Now, if I could only get my father to show up."

Chapter 27

Some women hang "Baby on Board" signs in their cars, but Mrs. James had a "Born to Shop" sign in her Volvo. Mrs. James had so many clothes that her closet looked like a sales rack; she had hundreds of items with the price tags still on them. Egypt learned to shop just like her mother. They could leave the house at 9:00 a.m. and not return until 9:00 p.m. Egypt loved shopping more than anything except Baby James. So, Mrs. James couldn't think of a better way to cheer up her daughter than to take her shopping for a dress for the debutante ball while Egypt's grandmother watched over Baby James at the hospital. Egypt sat up in her seat when her mother pulled into the mall entrance, which featured a sparkling waterfall surrounded by a bed of red dynasty tulips and yellow crown fritillarias.

After parking the car, Egypt and her mother walked into the

bookstore. Egypt almost walked past the children's section, but the giggles and laughter coming from that part of the store made her stop while her mother proceeded to the bargain books. She approached the kids and watched as they played with a train. The children connected the train cars, placed the train at the top of a hill, and gave it a push. The train flew down one hill and up another like a roller coaster at an amusement park. The children squealed with delight. Egypt couldn't believe she had created a child who might one day do the same thing.

Egypt joined her mother, who was examining the sale books near the front counter. She searched through the book section until she found *Geisha: A Life* by Mineko Iwasaki, a book about how the author was trained to entertain men in Japan. Paris had recommended it to her before the drama started in her life. She picked it up and handed the book to her mother, who had already gotten in the checkout line. As Egypt waited for her mother to complete the transaction, she stared into the mall entrance and watched as people walked past eating all kinds of food.

Mrs. James paid for the book and gave it to her daughter.

"Thank you, Mommy."

"You're welcome," replied Mrs. James as they walked out of the store.

"All of this food is making me hungry."

"I hope you're not pregnant again!" joked Mrs. James.

"No. I'm not sure I want to go through that again," said Egypt as they entered the food court.

"What do you want to eat?"

"I'm not sure."

"While you're deciding, I'm going to get some ice cream."

"OK."

Egypt scanned the food court and tried to figure out what she wanted. She thought about Chinese, but she didn't think it would fill her up. The burgers from Momma Burgers looked so juicy, with their sesame buns, lettuce, tomatoes, cheese, and ketchup dripping onto the tray. Alas, she had given up beef. She didn't have a taste for Big Al's greasy pizza either. Finally, the smell of fresh bread wafting from Carlo's Famous Italian Philadelphia Hoagies called her name.

The long line tested Egypt's resolve. But every time she thought about leaving, a person would come by with a hoagie with layers of meat sandwiched inside crusty Italian bread; the sight and smell of the delicious hoagie renewed her patience. Finally, Egypt reached the front of the line and approached the cashier, who was wearing a white paper hat and a striped shirt. Egypt looked up at the menu and ordered a turkey hoagie.

After a few minutes, Egypt retrieved her sandwich from the end of the counter. The cashier wrapped the large sandwich of wheat bread, turkey, American cheese, onions, green peppers, lettuce, tomatoes, mayo, pepper, and vinaigrette salad dressing in white butcher's paper. It sat cut in half on a paper plate on a red tray next to a cup of water.

Egypt picked up her tray and searched for her mother in the sea of square tables. When she spotted Mrs. James, she walked toward her until she saw a teenager in a red baseball cap standing in front of the carousel. She went to confront him, but he headed toward the ATM. She stopped and waited at a comfortable distance from him so as not to seem like a stalker. After he withdrew twenty dollars and put it in his wallet, she went up to him and tapped him on the shoulder.

William spun around in surprise. "Yikes! Are you following me?"

"No! What are you doing here?"

"I needed some cash."

"For your other baby mommas?"

"What are you talking about?"

"The doctor told me about all the girls you bring to the hospital."

William thought for a second. "Why aren't you with our child?"

"My mother wanted to give me a break from the hospital. We're going back to see him later, but I need you to answer my question before I let you see my son again."

"I'm going to see my son!" said William.

"Not if . . ." Egypt stopped in mid-sentence, putting her tray down on a table.

"What?" asked William.

"Not if you keep lying to me."

"I'm not lying," said William, prompting Egypt to bop him on the head. William put up his arms to block the blows. "I'll show you."

Egypt stopped beating William, stepped back, and folded her arms. "Let's go get tested, love," she said pointing to the mobile AIDS testing van parked on the outside of the food court.

"Let me think about it."

"Fine. Think about it while I eat my sandwich." While Egypt ate her hoagie, William checked his phone. Mrs. James walked up behind William as he texted, and signaled to her daughter to call her when she was finished. After she finished her hoagie, Egypt threw away her trash. She grabbed William, and they walked to the mobile testing unit, outside the mall. A long line of students from her high school was there. Egypt couldn't believe who she saw.

"Love, why are you here?" asked Egypt.

Paris dropped her head, ashamed of the answer. "I received a notice in the mail that the blood I gave at Eastside's blood drive tested positive for HIV."

"Oh my God! You have AIDS?"

Students turned around and looked at Egypt and Paris. "Can you keep it down?" asked Paris.

"I'm sorry, love" whispered Egypt.

"The samples were tainted, so I need to get tested again," said Paris.

Egypt grabbed Paris's hand. "How did this happen?"

"Remember what I told you about John?"

"That bastard!"

"Yeah . . . I found out that he has AIDS."

William walked up to Egypt and Paris. "What's going on?"

"We're all getting tested!" said Egypt.

Paris and William were too scared to do their consultation before their AIDS test, which involved talking to the health care worker at the testing table in the trailer. So Egypt volunteered to go first. She sat down in the chair. The young lady asked what brought her in today. Egypt told the nurse she had unprotected sex with somebody who had several partners. Egypt shot her eyes in William's direction and mentioned that she had just had a baby.

After telling Egypt about the AIDS test, the nurse took Egypt's hand, pricked the tip of her finger, dabbed it with some alcohol, and put a Band-Aid on it. Paris got her test after Egypt, but the girls had to drag William, who was kicking and screaming like a little baby, to the nurse's chair.

As the nurse conducted William's test, Egypt noticed he had dropped his phone on the floor. She picked it up, and a text message displayed on the screen. "Take the test and I'll take care of the rest, Baba."

Chapter 28

As Egypt sat in a white gown in the waiting room, she took off her white flat shoes, long white gloves, and tossed them across the room, where they landed near the coffee machine. She took off her fingernails and placed them on the table next to the chair. She pulled out the bobby pins that held her braids into a bun. Egypt removed her amulet of Bastet, earrings from her ears, and put them next to her other belongings. She wiped off her makeup with baby wipes. Egypt put her face into her hands until she heard her mother clear her throat. She looked up and saw an extremely handsome man standing next to Mrs. James.

He was tall, almost six feet, and wore a black tuxedo with a white shirt, a black vest, and a matching bow tie. He walked so softly into the room that Egypt barely heard his white patent leather shoes touching the floor. In his right hand, he carried a corsage in a plastic container. He had a boutonniere attached to his lapel, and his cuff links impressed Egypt; her father used to wear similar ones to church on Sunday.

His oval face reminded Egypt of William, and his caramel skin looked like a piece of wrapped candy. He had long, naturally curly hair that was pulled back into a ponytail.

As Egypt's mother approached, Egypt got up from her seat and grinned from ear to ear. "Who is this?" she asked.

"Your escort . . . from teenescort.com," Mrs. James replied.

"Oh my!" exclaimed Egypt.

Her escort approached Egypt, pinned the flower to her dress, and spoke in a deep voice. "I'm Prince."

"You sure are," blurted out Egypt.

Egypt, Mrs. James, and Prince all giggled. "I had almost forgotten about the debutante ball," said Egypt.

"That's why I told the limo driver to bring us to the hospital," said Mrs. James.

"Your mother told me you were gorgeous, but she didn't tell me I would be taking an African princess to the ball," Prince observed, lifting his eyebrows in appreciation.

"Stop it!" Egypt blushed.

"I mean it. You have the most beautiful complexion."

Mrs. James interrupted. "It's getting late. Y'all need to get going before you miss the entire affair."

"I can't," said Egypt, looking at Prince from head to toe. "Baby James is sick."

"Egypt, I will stay here and check on him," said Mrs. James.

"What if something happens?" asked Egypt.

"I'll call you."

Egypt sighed. "OK."

Mrs. James looked at Prince. "Take my daughter to the ball and make sure she gets her money's worth."

"I will," said Prince.

"Mom . . . He's not a gigolo."

"He should be," said her mother, laughing. "I'll stop if y'all go."

"Can I wear grandma's pearls?" asked Egypt.

"I almost forgot I had them," said Mrs. James as she took off the pearls and put them around Egypt's neck.

Egypt grabbed Prince by the arm, and they headed out of the hospital. When they reached the entrance, they saw a white stretch limousine parked near the door. Egypt stopped on the sidewalk in front of the limousine while the driver held the door open. Prince guided her into the vehicle and then followed as the driver closed the door.

The limo driver began driving to the Fox Theatre, the location of the debutante ball. Egypt sat next to Prince with her legs crossed and her hands together. "This is cleaner than my grandfather's car," Egypt said, "and his car is spotless."

"The Rolls-Royce limo is the best," said Prince as he leaned back.

"How many limousines have you been in?"

"I can't remember."

A text popped up on Egypt's phone, and she typed a response.

"Who was that?" asked Prince

"Paris, my best friend. She's already at the debutante ball and she was just checking on me," said Egypt as she placed her phone on the mini bar. "Do you take girls to a lot of events?"

The vehicle stopped on Peachtree Street in front of the theater's neon sign. "I'll tell you later," said Prince as the driver opened the limo door outside of the Fabulous Fox Theatre, built for the Shriners in the 1920s. The marquee displayed a message: "Welcome to an Enchanted Evening with the Pharaohs."

After stepping out of the limousine, the couple walked toward the entrance holding hands. Egypt and Prince tried to enter the main doors of the theater, but employees in red jackets directed them to the side entrance, which led into the Egyptian Ballroom.

Adorned with extensive columns and decorations, the Egyptian Ballroom provided the perfect mystique for the ball. It resembled a temple at Karnak for Ramses II, also known as Ramses the Great. At the temple, Ramses the Great had numerous statues built in his image, more than any other pharaoh. In addition, the bathroom on the lower level featured reproductions of Tutankhamun's God Throne, discovered by Howard Carter in 1922 in the antechamber, the first room of King Tut's tomb.

Egypt and Prince walked through the entrance to the Egyptian Ballroom. Escorts dressed in tuxedos and debutantes in white gowns wearing long white gloves, were lined up behind several tables in between columns covered in hieroglyphs. India was leaning against a column with her girlfriend, wearing high tops, shorts, and a basketball jersey.

Egypt looked over at her. "What are you doing here?"

"I'm a debutante, too," replied India.

"You didn't earn enough money for the scholarship, remember?"

India steamed. "I'll whoop your . . ." she started, but before she could finish, one of the sorority sisters escorted her out of the ballroom.

"Who was that?" asked Prince.

"Nobody," said Egypt. "Let's check in."

When the couple got to the table, Egypt handed Paris her ID, who smiled at her best friend.

"You got a good one—not like my escort," said Paris.

"He's very nice," said Egypt as she introduced Prince. "What happened to yours?"

"He's in the bathroom, powdering his nose," said Paris disdainfully. "Where are you white gloves?"

"I left them at the hospital," replied Egypt.

"I'll get you a pair."

Egypt's stomach growled. The smell of food had reached her nose. She grabbed Prince and dragged him toward the buffet line. As they reached the table, Egypt picked up a plate and started dumping food on it: fresh spinach with French dressing, spring rolls, green beans, meatballs, chicken fingers, pasta salad, and sliced turkey. Egypt guided Prince to a dining table and they sat down. Egypt said a blessing and prayer for her son.

"That's a lot of food," said Prince as Egypt began stuffing herself.

"I'm starving," she said between bites. "I've been at the hospital all day and I haven't eaten a thing."

Prince cut a few pieces of turkey and put them into his mouth. "Your mom told me the baby has been sick," he said.

"Yeah," said Egypt, "he's had an infection and the doctors are trying to treat it."

"Is he going to be OK?"

"He's a preemie, but he's strong," Egypt replied. They cleaned their plates and drank some water.

Paris walked up behind Egypt and handed her a brand-new pair of long white gloves. She slipped them on as the mistress of ceremonies approached the podium and welcomed the audience to the debutante ball, the introduction of the young ladies to society. After a few announcements, she invited the debutantes to the stage for the dance with their escorts.

"How do you know the dance?" Egypt whispered in Prince's ear.

"I actually went to dancing etiquette for boys and they taught us the dance."

As Egypt exited the dance floor, she spotted her father standing in the back of the room, dressed in a black tuxedo. She told Prince she had to go to the bathroom as he headed toward their table. Egypt walked slowly toward her father, and when she reached him, she hugged him as tightly as she could; she couldn't believe he had made it.

Egypt let him go and wiped her eyes. "How did you know?"

"I am always watching you, even when you don't see," he replied, smiling at her.

The mistress of ceremonies came to the stage to announce that it was time for the father-daughter dance. Egypt and Mr. James joined the other fathers and daughters in the highlight of the evening. Mr. James offered Egypt his arm, and she held onto it with her white gloves as they made a grand entrance to the dance floor. The other father-daughter pairs walked in line behind them. As Egypt curtsied and Mr. James bowed, the audience recognized her father as the head of the LD03. The other pairs cleared the center of the dance floor, leaving the spotlight on Egypt and Mr. James.

Mr. James pulled out his handkerchief and placed it in his right hand so his palm wouldn't graze Egypt's back. The Tuxedo band played the Chicago Glide, the waltz of the ball. Egypt grabbed her father's left hand as he placed his right one on the small of her back. Mr. James moved forward with his left patent leather shoe and slid to the right; Egypt moved back with her right flat shoe and slid with her left. They finished the sequence when Mr. James closed his right foot and Egypt closed her left. They continued the rise-and-fall movements for what seemed like forever; even then, the girl continued to enjoy the dance with her father.

The audience erupted in applause as the fathers finished their first sequence of the dance and the escorts stood around the edge of the dance floor. The debutantes curtsied to their fathers again in exchange for the men's bows. Mr. James and the other fathers placed their right hands on the small of their daughter's backs and held their left, spinning the girls several times. At the end of the dance, each pairing hugged and left the dance floor, one behind the other.

Egypt and Mrs. James took their seats at the table. "Thank you for coming, love" Egypt said as she grabbed her father's hand and looked into his eyes.

"I couldn't miss your debut into society," Mr. James responded.

"But you've already missed so much. Why tonight?"

"It was time."

"Daddy," Egypt spoke in a little girl's voice.

"Yes, sweetheart," replied Mr. James fondly.

"I've wanted to tell you something for a long time."

"What is it?"

"I'm sorry for standing you up on our daughter–Daddy Date when I was nine."

"That was a long time ago."

"But that's the reason you left us."

Mr. James laughed. "That couldn't be further from the truth."

"Why did you leave then?" Egypt asked.

"It's complicated. I didn't like what I had become, and your mother and I decided that it would be best if I wasn't around you."

"Why not?"

"I have a problem."

"What?" asked Egypt.

"I think you know what I'm talking about," replied Mr. James.

"Have you been getting help?"

"Yes. That's the reason that I came tonight."

"So, you can come home then?" asked Egypt.

"That's not possible," replied Mr. James.

"Why not?"

Mr. James looked around the room to see all the people staring at them. "There are some things that I have no control over," he whispered.

"Like the LD03?" Egypt mumbled as she felt a tap on her shoulder. She turned to see Paris crying. "Love, what's going on?" she questioned.

"Did you leave your cell phone in the limo?" Paris asked.

"Yes," Egypt nodded. "I forgot it by mistake."

"Your mother has been trying to call you," said Paris.

"Why? Is something wrong?"

"Baby James . . ."

Chapter 29

The James family walked into the fellowship hall for the repast and assembled around the head table, which extended the length of the room. Egypt, wearing a black dress, a black hat, and sunglasses, stood next to her mother, holding her hand. The pastor tried to talk into the microphone, but no sound came out. Suddenly, a yellow jacket buzzed around Egypt and stung her. After wheezing for a moment, she fell to the floor. Mrs. James and the rest of the family ran to her aid. Her mother opened Egypt's purse, pulled out her EpiPen, and jammed it into her thigh. After a few moments, she woke up.

"Oh my God," said Egypt. "What happened?"

"You were stung," replied Mrs. James as she sighed, and exclamations of "Praise the Lord," "Amen," "Bless your heart," and "Hallelujah" filled the room for one of the church's favorite daughters. Egypt had grown up in the church. Her singing often brought tears to the eyes of people who heard her on Sunday morning, and her dances were the highlight of Women's Day. Ladies in the kitchen would stop cooking just to see her perform.

As the women of the church continued to take care of Egypt, Sister Jordan pulled the foil off the trays of collard greens, beans, rice, baked chicken, ham, turkey, and macaroni and cheese, and lit the gas canisters to heat the food. She placed straw baskets at the end of the table and opened a bag of rolls. She poured the rolls into the basket, threw the plastic bag into the trash can, and put a serving spoon into each pan. Mourners from the funeral and burial got in line and waited for the pastor to bless the food.

The janitor walked into the room with a new PA system. He plugged the equipment into the wall and tested the microphone, but no sound came out. He turned a few dials, but there was still no sound. He left the room, returned with a mic, and plugged it in. It worked, but the feedback hurt everybody's ears until he turned it down to a bearable level and pulled down the microphone so it would be at the right height for the pastor.

Around this time, a member of the church checked on Egypt and gave her a cold compress. Egypt sat up and said, "I feel better."

"I think she'll be fine," said the church member, "but can somebody get her some water?"

Sagmus ran to the kitchen, grabbed a few bottles of water from the counter, and handed her cousin one of them. Egypt took a couple of sips. "Thank you."

"We can take you home if you don't want to stay," said Mrs. James.

"No, I want to be around family," said Egypt as the nurse helped her to a seat at the table. Mrs. James leaned over to the pastor and whispered in his ear. He walked up to the podium, opened his Bible, and flipped through a few pages. He stopped at a verse, Matthew 19:24, and began praying, giving the longest blessing Egypt had ever heard. She closed her eyes as tight as she could and listened to each and every word, hoping the pastor's words would ease the pain of losing Baby James.

Immediately following the prayer, the United Methodist women served the James family. The women had decorated the tables of the fellowship hall with white tablecloths and blue flowers that surrounded a centerpiece of a glass vase with a candle floating inside. The women had placed coffee cups around the table settings. Sister Thomas walked in from the kitchen and dumped a bag of ice into the lemonade. Sister Powell placed the deviled eggs around a platter so perfectly that it looked like a piece of art. The blinds were open, and sunlight streamed into the room, trying to shine light on a heartbreak that tested the faith of the entire congregation.

As people stood in the buffet line, Egypt sat at the family table and picked at her baked chicken, rice with giblet gravy, and green beans.

Out of nowhere, India came up to Egypt. "I'm sorry you lost your baby," said India as she reached out her hand to Egypt.

Egypt grabbed it incredulously but relaxed after feeling the sincerity in her touch. "Thank you," said Egypt.

"My little brother died last year," said India.

"I'm sorry," said Egypt.

"Yeah . . . he only lived a few hours."

"At least I had Baby James for a couple of weeks . . ."

"Probably seems like a lifetime."

"It does."

"I'm going back to my seat now."

"Thanks for coming by."

"No problem."

As India left to join her sister, Egypt's eyes roamed around the room in search of Paris. There were people everywhere, but there was no sign of her BFF. She saw people lining up to use the bathroom. Men were dragging extra chairs out of the stockroom because so many people had come to the repast. The pastor had to run the children off the old piano to keep them from banging out dissonant melodies. The garbage cans began to overflow, paper plates tumbling to the floor.

Finally, after searching for a few minutes, she spotted a crowd of people surrounding a table, signing cards. As Egypt stood up from her chair, she could see a teenager in a long dress: her best friend. Paris was having people sign the guest book. Egypt smiled, and her mother pulled her back down to her seat.

"Who are you looking for?" asked Mrs. James.

"Paris," said Egypt.

"I saw her helping with the registrar."

"Nobody can replace a friend," said Egypt, still looking at the table. When Paris's and Egypt's eyes met, they waved at each other. A church member tapped Paris on the shoulder and took over supervising the signing of the guest book. Paris walked toward the

James family's table. Egypt got out of her chair and started walking toward Paris. They met in the middle of the room and hugged.

"I knew I could count on you, love," said Egypt, looking into Paris's eyes with affection.

"That's what friends are for," said Paris. "Your shoes are cute."

Egypt lifted up her sunglasses and wiped her eyes. "Your hair is beautiful."

"Thank you," said Paris. "Are you OK?"

Egypt sighed. "Love, how am I going to make it?"

"One day at time and with a little payback."

"What are you talking about? . . . Paris?"

"It's time to implement the plan."

CHAPTER 30

John walked around the tables in the cafeteria, holding a protest sign and hollering, "No Justice! No Peace!" to protest the closure of the senior hall. The administrator had closed the area during Spirit Week after the seniors poured baby oil on the floors and several teachers slipped and fell. Their actions interrupted John's illegal pharmaceutical business, and he became the lone iconoclast left of the LD03 since the rest of them had been sent to alternative school. His campaign captured the students' attention; they stopped eating to watch. However, security officers showed up and physically removed him.

After the commotion, Stephen slid down the breakfast line and told the server in a dull voice that he wanted ham, a biscuit, some grits, and a carton of orange juice. The server placed the food on his tray, and he waited to pay for his breakfast. The student in front of him claimed he had forgotten his lunch money, and the lunch lady fussed at him so much that Stephen started shaking and couldn't remember his meal number. The other students started calling him dumb, until India got up from her seat in the cafeteria and approached the lunch counter. The boys shut up just as if a marine sergeant had given them an order. India's act of kindness seemed to jolt Stephen's brain, because he remembered his password and typed it into the panel.

India walked back to her seat and resumed reading her Bible. Stephen stood at the front of the line looking around the cafeteria, but he didn't see anybody he wanted to eat with. He finally decided to sit with India. After pulling out a chair, Stephen sat down and cut up his ham into two pieces to make a sandwich with his biscuit. He took two bites before swallowing the entire thing. He pushed the ends of his orange juice container open and drank its contents all at once.

As India read, the curmudgeonly principal of Eastside High School walked up.

India glared at her. "Can I help you?"

The principal threw her arms up into the air. "I can't believe you read the Bible."

"What are you trying to say?"

"I think you know."

Stephen stopped eating and jumped up from his seat, hearing a lack of respect in the principal's voice. "Apologize!"

The stunned principal mumbled, "I'm sorry."

India interjected. "Stephen, sit down; I can take care of myself."

Stephen returned to his chair with his eyes locked on the principal; she had always cultivated a stoic image, but Stephen had shattered her nerves. The principal looked dazed until a call came over her walkie-talkie. He reached down to his belt and tried to pull it out of the holder, but it dropped to the floor. As he struggled to pick it up, he could feel the rumbling of students stampeding out of the cafeteria as the school bell rang for classes to begin.

A natural reaction came over India; she knew she had better move or get trampled. Stephen helped her out. He picked her up and carried her out of the cafeteria. As India looked back, she could see the principal struggle to get to her feet, as students kept kicking the walkie-talkie. When Stephen and India got into the hallway, he put her down as students ran past them. She turned around and kissed him for what seemed like forever to Stephen. Their lips broke apart; India opened her eyes, but Stephen stood in the middle of the hall with his eyes closed. India cleared her throat.

Stephen opened his eyes and smiled.

"Did you enjoy it?" asked India.

"Yes," replied Stephen. "But I thought you were . . ."

"I'm not what you think I am."

India grabbed Stephen by the hand and took him outside the building, near the bus lane, where they met up with Egypt and Paris. They could see everybody staring at the trees—toilet paper hung from the limbs in front of the school. The discipline administrator had borrowed a rake from the janitor. He tried to grab a piece of paper on a limb, but he fell flat on his face in the grass, and the rake landed in front of him. Egypt, Paris, India, and Stephen burst out laughing.

In the bus lane, the attendance principal tried to remove the tires that were blocking the entrance of the school. They were stacked on top of one another like the tires in a store. As he tried to move them, students started rolling more tires down the hill. The bus drivers and the administrators became part of a dodgeball game using tires. The girls and Stephen laughed so hard that tears rolled down their faces.

"It's good to see you laugh," said Paris.

"Oh my God," said Egypt. "I didn't even realize it."

But Egypt stopped smiling when she saw William sitting on his motorcycle next to the ninth graders rolling tires down the hill. Something came over her. She left Paris, India, and Stephen and walked over to William. Before she knew it, she had pushed him over into the street. The students went crazy laughing. Egypt walked back over to her group and dusted off her hands.

"Totally awesome," said Paris.

"Thanks for the comment, love," replied Egypt. "It's time to implement your plan."

"Have you thought how you are going to get William to fall for the Legend of the Swimming Pool?" asked Paris.

Egypt removed her book bag from her shoulder and placed it on the ground. She unzipped it and pulled out a notecard embossed with an image of Bastet. "Give him this card, and don't forget to text my uncle."

"Got it," said Paris as she walked toward William, who was still struggling to pick up his motorcycle with the crowd jeering at him. Egypt headed toward the weight room; actually, there was no swimming pool at Eastside. Yet Senior Last Will and Testaments often raved about the "Legend of the Swimming Pool," when the greatest parties of all time took place. Seniors would tell freshmen that the school had a pool party on the first Friday of the school year and would get them to dress in their swimsuits; the scrubs walked around the school all day looking for the nonexistent pool. Paris and Egypt decided to introduce William to a new angle of the legend.

William opened the door to the weight room and saw Egypt sitting on a workout bench. He walked over to her and started firing off questions at her in a demanding voice. "Do you think I would fall for that freshman prank? What have you done with my letter?"

Egypt stood up and looked him in the eye. "It was worth a try."

"If you don't give me my results . . ."

"Hold up," said Egypt as she raised her voice. "Who do you think you're talking to?"

"A little girl," said William.

"Love, not anymore—thanks to you."

"That doesn't matter. Why did the health department give you my results?"

"When I picked up my report, they asked me if I knew how to contact you, because your letter came back to them."

"We moved."

"I told them we were sex partners, and I knew how to contact you. So they gave it to me."

"Will you hand it over?"

Egypt reached into her book bag and handed him the letter. He tore off the short end of the envelope, pulled out the paper, and read it.

"I don't have it," said William as he jumped for joy, but when he read more of the information, his smile turned upside down.

"Why does the letter say a negative result doesn't mean I don't have AIDS?"

"We have to get tested every six months because you slept with Lisa," replied Egypt.

"She has AIDS?" asked William.

"Yes," replied Egypt.

"What about her baby?"

"They used drugs to prevent AIDS from spreading to the child."

"Great!"

"I wish you had been that concerned about Baby James when he was alive."

"I loved our child!" William cried. "Part of me died when Baby James passed away," he added as he wiped the tears from his eyes."

"Sorry for assuming you didn't care about our baby," said Egypt. "But why do you get girls pregnant?"

"Trying to prove to my father I was a man."

William sighed as the door burst open and the police ran in. They hurried over to him, wrestled him to the ground, and put handcuffs on his wrists.

"Yikes!" cried William. "Why are you arresting me?"

"Mostly for being a stupid teenager," replied Egypt's uncle as he pulled a lollipop out of his mouth. "But you and the LD03 are being charged with human trafficking."

As the police dragged William away, Egypt gave her uncle a hug.

"I'm glad you and Paris included me in your plan," said Uncle Terry. "This will shut down part of the LD03's operations."

"There's more?" asked Egypt.

"William is just a little fish."

Chapter 31

Egypt and Paris leaned against the back wall of the gym, watching the teachers cover the gym floor with a black tarp. The junior class had decorated the gym for the baccalaureate ceremony, setting up chairs and hanging banners. Egypt and Paris had placed tropical flowers in front of the podium. The cameraman finally found the perfect place to take pictures next to the band, who were tuning up their instruments. The principal and her administration appeared on stage in caps and gowns. The band director raised his baton, and the band began playing music.

The people in the audience stood up, and the graduates marched into the gym, the girls wearing gold gowns and the boys wearing black.

After the graduates had been seated, the security guards opened the doors and latecomers thundered into the gym; men, women, and children stomped up the stairs like a stampede of horses.. Egypt and Paris ran to their seats in the last row of the graduates.

Finally, the program began. The principal asked the audience to stand for the presentation of the colors by the ROTC—one of the most decorated units in the state. The Air Force ROTC color guard marched down the center of the aisle to take their place in front of the podium. After the guard presented the colors, a student sang the national anthem a cappella. The crowd clapped as the color guard marched out of the gym.

"You all may be seated," said the principal.

"I hope the speaker doesn't talk too long," Egypt whispered to Paris as the class president spoke.

Paris turned to Egypt. "I thought you enjoyed hearing the word."

"Love, it doesn't take me three hours to feel the spirit," joked Egypt.

The girls turned their attention to the stage, where members of the choir prepared to sing. Several girls and boys from the senior class got up from their seats and walked to the stage. Three different microphones were set up. The girls huddled around one microphone and the boys gathered around the other. India approached the microphone in the middle. The crowd cheered itself into a frenzy.

Egypt leaned over to Paris. "I didn't know India could sing!"

"Before her family became homeless, she sang at all the assemblies in ninth grade," Paris responded.

The clamor of the crowd began to subside as India adjusted the microphone and tested it. "Check one, two." India gave a testimony. "I would like to thank the graduating class for inviting me to sing with them." Claps came from the audience. "Life has dealt my family a difficult hand, but things are getting better."

The graduates, the audience, Egypt, and Paris stood up and gave India a rousing ovation. When the crowd finally sat down, India began to sing a song most of the audience knew from church, "I Feel Like Going On." As India sang, everyone sang along. By the time she finished, there wasn't a dry eye in the gymnasium.

Next, a speaker got up and delivered a sermon. After about ten minutes of her message, Paris elbowed Egypt in her side.

"Ouch! . . . Why did you poke me?" asked Egypt, clutching her stomach.

"We have to go get ready to serve the seniors and their families."

The girls quietly got up and snuck down to the cafeteria, where the reception was being held. Janitors had set up tables; a rainbow of gold balloons connected each table to the center table, making a passageway so the guests could walk through. Gold tablecloths covered each table, along with a silver punch bowl, clear plastic cups, and gold napkins with "Eastside High School" printed on them.

After the ceremony, Egypt, Paris, and the junior class officers served the students and parents cookies, cakes, chips, petits fours, finger sandwiches, chicken wings, and punch. As Egypt's table cleared of guests, she saw India standing alone. So she walked over to her.

"That was one of the most beautiful songs I ever heard," said Egypt.

"Thank you," said India in a soft voice.

"Why did you stop singing?"

"I didn't think I had anything to sing about after we lost everything."

Paris ran up behind Egypt, and India and hugged them like they were buddies.

"Why are y'all being so nice to me?" asked India, shrugging her off. "None of you like me!"

Egypt smiled. "We don't hate you either. We just need to get to know each other better."

"I'd like that," said India.

"And that's the best sermon of the day," said Paris. "Besides . . ."

"What?" asked Egypt.

"Mr. G isn't going to jail."

"Why not?" asked India.

"I'm not going to testify, so they have no case," said Paris. "But Mr. G. agreed not to teach in the United States ever again. So the DA decided to drop the charges."

"I have some good news, too," said India with a grin. "The United Methodist Church has found us a temporary house until my mother gets a job."

"Great!" said Egypt. "My turn."

"Shoot," said Paris.

"I'm attending a summer program at Clark Atlanta University."

"Me too!" said Paris. They all took their hands in excitement and danced around the room.

About the Author

Steven Thedford began his writing career by winning a writing contest at Build Academy in Buffalo, New York for a book about an Easter egg in elementary school. His talents always amazed his fellow students. For instance, during the reading of a poem in a high school English class, he began a poem by saying, "I have the taste of the past in my mouth." But before he could continue, a fellow classmate hollered out, "You didn't write that."

With guidance from Dawn Scotland, a professor at Clark College, now Clark Atlanta University, Thedford polished his skills and won third place in a national essay contest honoring Dr. Marin Luther King, Jr., during his freshman year of college. He further used his abilities as a graduate student to write articles for a school newsletter. Moreover, during this time at North Carolina

State University he published his own newsletter, African Expressions, a publication of poems.

After graduate school, Thedford taught math and physics at Mbeji Academy in Ngi'ya Kenya, East Africa, as a fellow of the International Foundation of Education and Self Help. The experience inspired him to enter the teaching field in which he has nurtured young minds at Kennedy Middle School in Charlotte, North Carolina, Redan High School in Stone Mountain, Georgia, and DeKalb Online Academy in Decatur, Georgia. Presently, Thedford teaches physics at Arabia Mountain High School in Lithonia, GA.

Thedford participated in a summer Teacher's Intern Program sponsored by the University of North Carolina at Charlotte's Department of Education, where he conducted research on Celgard® membranes (Hoechst-Celanese). He also worked in the corporate section and as a civilian for the armed services—namely, Xerox Corporation, the Naval Ocean System Center (NOSCS), Honeywell Corporation, the Naval Surface Warfare Center, the Centers for Disease Control, and the Georgia Institute of Technology.

In 2015 his fellow teachers at Dekab Online Academy selected him as the "Teacher of the Year." Students have nominated him for "Who's Who Among American High School Teachers" for five different years. In addition, Thedford has been a Tandy Technology School Scholar and a National Institute of Health Apprentice and was selected to participate in the NanoTeach Pilot Program and Georgia Industrial Fellowship for Teachers. Finally, the University of Georgia honored Thedford with the Teacher of Promise Award.

Using his experiences, Thedford published his first book *Inquiry Based Science Activities and Internet Lessons*. New World Press, Inc. published Thedford's second book, *The Kwanzaa Coloring Book (Games and Puzzles)*, which introduces children to the principles and symbols of the African American holiday of Kwanzaa. Moreover, New World Press, Inc., published Thedford's poetry book *Nobody Told Me It Was Like This*, "poetry you can understand." Furthermore, in 2019 Thedford released *Kwanzaa Gets an A*, a picture book about the history of Kwanzaa and why the name has two a's. Finally, Thedford will released his second book of poetry in December of 2020, *Kwansabas and Other Poems*, an art form based on the South African praise poem.

CPSIA information can be obtained
at www.ICGtesting.com
Printed in the USA
BVHW031926240222
629844BV00008B/26/J